THE
WEAVE OF
MY LIFE

Elsa Rosenvasser Feher

ISBN: 979-8698783633

To GF

I had the élan; you had the self-confidence.
I was your rainbow; you were my rock.
Together, we galloped.

Contents

The weave

Prologue (january 2019)

How to render meaningful 75 years of journals at the end of one's life? I don't want them to go unacknowledged. They have, after all, been with me and multiplied throughout all this time. But on starting to reread them, I found myself writing another journal entry and so starting a Journal of Journals. That won't do, no.

My journals record thoughts and feelings more than actual happenings. But still, they provide a timeline to a life. So today at the beach — where I do my best thinking — I thought that I could try using the journals as source material for writing life stories I wanted to tell. The journals would serve as historical background as I re-examined my life thematically. In other words, instead of choosing a linear approach to the narrative, following the journals and the flow of time, I'd use a different organizing principle: life as a web, a grid, a weave.

The weave as organizing metaphor. A weave is a two-dimensional affair: in its simplest form, it consists of a set of parallel threads and another set of threads that traverse the first set. The number of threads per square inch is a measure of the looseness or tightness of the weave. In the metaphor, where the woven fabric represents my life, the weave becomes tighter as the years go by: in a long life like mine, the number of threads per square inch gets high, as in a good-quality fabric. My task, then, is to take some thread, or yarn, and weave my life into a fabric, perhaps a tapestry.

The first step a weaver takes is laying the warp. The warp is the first set of threads — or strands of yarn. The strands run parallel in a rectangular loom, or along diameters if I choose a circular design. The loom holds the warp strands taut. The weft is made up of strands woven over and under the warp. The crisscrossing threads make up the fabric or tapestry.

So what are the warp and weft in the fabric of my life? The warp is the infrastructure, the base of the fabric. It is under tension, so its strands must be strong. In my metaphor, this infrastructure is what I bring with me, the essential me, who I am, my identity. It is my foundation, what is strong and durable in me.

The weft can be fanciful, creating designs according to the pattern of criss-crossings. It is what fills out and gives texture to the fabric. In my metaphor, the weft is made up of the stories I've lived, the tales I tell. By necessity, they always traverse aspects of my identity, my warp. Every time they do so, the stories add nuance to what is already there, they illuminate it further. Mostly, the stories, the weft, are accounts of happenings, and reflections on times, places, and people.

In the eight chapters that follow, the first four are the warp of my weave and the remaining four are the weft. The weft could be made denser by adding more life stories, but for now these will have to suffice. The text, written at age 86, is punctuated with entries from my journals; to deduce my age when I wrote a particular journal entry, please note I was born in december 1932. In addition to journal excerpts, I've interspersed related articles and essays I've written in previous years on similar topics.

The scene behind the loom

Writing the stories and essays is the easy part, or at least it is straightforward. But a myriad of questions arise when one wants to make it into an 'exportable item'; that is, a product with its own tenable independent existence, a book. Here are a few:

Language. Spanish or english, which should it be? This is an old conundrum. My friend Marguerite Dorian faced it when she settled in the USA and she chose to write in english over french and romanian; Kafka chose german over czech; Conrad chose english over polish; our friends, the israeli poets Tuvia Rübner and Dan Pagis, took up hebrew, and gave up, respectively, german and romanian. Most of these decisions were excruciating. They involved circumstances in which the writers felt forced to abandon their mother tongue if they were going to have readers. For myself, it is nothing so extreme. I simply have to acknowledge that my family reads english with much more ease than spanish. So I opt for english but, unrealistically (my time on Earth is not infinite), I don't abandon the idea of eventually doing a weave in spanish — for I love writing in the tongue that ties me to my early years. It is as Maria Elena Walsh, argentinian chansonnière, sings to her motherland about one reason she wants to live there: "… porque el idioma de la infancia es un secreto entre las dos" (… because the language of my childhood is a secret between us).

Style. As you've probably noticed by now, I prefer lowercase to capital letters. The excess of capitalization (use of uppercase letters) in english strikes me as so … gothic-germanic-script-ish. I prefer the flow of lower case, the lack of hierarchies of the latin languages. So I figured that I can give up writing in the spanish language, but I don't have to give up some of its characteristics. Therefore, you will find that I only use capital letters for proper names: people, countries, rivers, and mountains. I do not capitalize nationalities. My computer's self-correct feature — which I abhor — gives me a hard time with this. But I insist.

Someone once wrote, "You have the right to capitalize, and I have the right to lower case." In fact, the further back in time you go, the more common the use of capital letters; present-day tendency toward lower case reflects a less formal, less hierarchical society. My personal preference goes back to e. e. cummings in the early 1950s. When Hector Rubinstein and I got married in 1956, our wedding announcement was a card showing a Paul Klee drawing of little people in a boat, with its caption: 'à contre-courànt sous la pleine lune' ('against the current under a full moon'). The caption and all else — our names, place of the event, date — was printed in lower case. Now, 60 years later, I go back to that preference. The south african poet Ante Krog said, "I distrust anything that starts with a capital letter and ends with a full stop," and proceeded to write poetry in a style she did not have to distrust. In a similar vein I now set my own style, a style that I like and trust. So long as I am consistent and clear, why not?

Initials instead of names. On occasion, people who appear in the narrative are identified by their initials. Such is the case of my husband George, who appears as GF. How could I refer to him as George when I never, ever called him so? He was Gyuri, Gyurika, Spiva, Spivale. In my early diaries he was GF, later simplified to G or Gy. But never George. Hence, GF he remains. Similarly, my first husband, Hector Rubinstein, appears as HRR, as he did in my journals.

Coding the diaries. I started keeping journals at age 12. When I peruse them now I find that sometimes there are entries almost daily, sometimes for long periods there are none at all — usually when life is moving along peacefully. The last few years I haven't had the benefit of chatting with GF, so the entries are usually essays on books or current events — subject-matter I would have talked over with him. It was not a simple task to find the journal nuggets that are now scattered throughout the weave (the bits in italics). It meant reading those journal pages and identifying the portions that were meaningful for my weave: events, people, moods, philosophy of life. Having parsed the content into categories, I assigned colors to them, bought a whole stash of colored stickums, and waded through the journals again, placing the stickums to color-code the topics. Messy, laborious, not unlike data analysis in field research. But fun, often intriguing, and sometimes disturbing, as I read long-forgotten entries.

Epilogue (march 2020)

Prior to sending this off for publication, I reread the chapters written this past year and found some of them are branded by the desolation and grief and longing I felt over my loss of GF. That is as it should be; they are a testament to the time in which they were written.

Now, one year after embarking on this weaving project, I find an unexpected payoff. Ever since GF died in 2017 I had the feeling that I was like the Titanic after hitting the iceberg: sinking because I carried so much life within me. I felt my life had been so full, full to the brim, that it was drowning me. It was as if I didn't want more life — the so-called additional life that had been granted me in my widowhood was not what I wanted.

Then I started writing, weaving stories out of my recollections, reading old journals to remember things forgotten that illuminate the present. And, miraculously, I find I'm no longer sinking. The load grows lighter as I weave. Each new strand I write feels like cargo being thrown overboard so my load of life is lessened. The image that comes to mind is of a precious rug, woven so dense that it floats my lived life back to the surface. An unexpected payoff and a lifesaver, to be sure.

Laying the warp

In the metaphor of life as a woven fabric, a tapestry, the warp is the underpinning of the life edifice. One can think about its strands as passport-type information: gender, nationality, citizenship, and in olden times (not so distant), also religion and race. Essentially, it is identity; in my case, the distillation of a lifetime of answers to questions like these:

Are you first a woman or a jew?
You are american: north american or south american?
Do you consider yourself to be primarily a scientist?

The answer depends on who is asking. And my answers probably have varied over time as my priorities changed.

Today, to define myself and lay my warp, I say this:

> I am a woman
>
> I am american: I live in North America,
> grew up in South America
>
> I am a rational thinker: I deal with ideas
>
> I am jewish

Among these strands I do not assign priorities; no one trait has more weight than the others. But because a write-up is linear, the warp strands of needs appear in a certain order in this document.

And yet … there is a kind of timeline, and therefore an underlying order, even if it is not an order of importance within my sense of identity. Let me explain, as I take the strands one by one.

I am a woman: the feminist strand that shaped me goes back only about 60 years, counting from the origins of the Beauvoir-Friedan-Steinem movement, or 100, if we go back to the suffragists.

I am american: the american identity strand goes back 500 years, if we count from the arrival of the european settlers, or 200, if we count from the independence of the new nations and their quest for self-determination.

I am a rational thinker: the rational mind goes hand-in-hand with western thought. It first appeared over 2,000 years ago in the greek way of questioning the world, asking not only 'how?' but 'why?' To be — as I aspired to be — a physicist in the 1950s was equivalent, in my mind, to being a philosopher in ancient Greece, a talmudist in the 10th century, a cartesian thinker in the 17th century.

I am jewish: the jewish tradition, based on the Jewish Bible (or Old Testament), takes me back to the beginnings of time, close to 6,000 years according to The Book. I've decided to let the warp strands appear in an order consistent with this chronology, indicating that I belong both to the very old and to the somewhat new.

On being a woman

In my father's library

I learnt to read by myself, crawling along the floor of my father's study and pulling out volumes from the lowest shelf of his library. I was probably about three years old, and this is my very first recollection.

My father's library was voluminous. There were no public libraries in Buenos Aires where one could borrow books. So buying books and building one's own library was every intellectual's task. It meant all sorts of books were on hand at home. Over my 23 years in my parents' home I would roam the rooms and pull out books to suit my mood or interest at the moment. One day, when I was a teenager, I pulled out 'Sex and Character' by Otto Weininger. The effect of reading it was stupefying.

Weininger, whose book caused a furor when it was published in 1903, was undeniably a misogynist. (Strindberg loved his work.) I was of an age when a paramount question was: what does it mean to be a woman in — as it was becoming clearer to me by the day — a man's world? So the title of the book appealed to me. But the contents were very disturbing. In his tirade against women, Weininger's contention was that they are inferior beings, amoral, alogical, and incapable of 'mental excitement.' This, and much else that he argued, went against every fiber of my being, every belief about myself, everything I felt and knew. What was such a book doing in my father's library? Surely he did not agree with or condone such ideas?

My recollection of this reaction is so strong that I thought surely it must be recorded in my diaries. I remembered writing about it at the time. When I could not find it in my journals it occurred to me I had written an essay for school about the topic. It turns out I have kept a couple of notebooks with essays and I find, sure enough, one, in english, titled 'Women's careers.' I was 16 at the time. But, surprise! I have conflated memories. The essay was based on a careful reading of another book in my father's library, this one by George Simmel, a not-objectionable german sociologist of the early 1900s. My recollection is that the topic was so important to me that I took one whole week during Easter vacation to read and ponder the book and write the essay. I find (in Google, where else?) some present-day erudite writings saying that Simmel's writings on women were not much appreciated until the 1970s. The school essay is from 1948: *Simmel tells us that "the general forms of poetry are creations of man, and as the specifically feminine poetic forms, although possible, are still left to the regions of utopia, at least for the time being, there is a slight contradiction in trying to fill masculine forms with feminine contents. Indeed, if the feminine soul, so different from the masculine one, tried to express itself in the same manner, there would be an immediate disagreement between the traditional lyrical style and the feeling." However … women have been found to achieve important work in the field of mathematics because in the subject there is no chance for feminine and masculine intellect to have different reactions as it is purely objective and the facts are presented without interference of the exhibitor's feelings or opinions.*

The essay continues to consider the writing of novels, music, medicine … and concludes: *But we do not doubt women's capacity and believe the feminine work will succeed in riding on a basis of its own without the need of adapting itself to the masculine pattern.* The essay received a score of 9 out of 10. Of course, my school was a girls-only school.

Women role-models in a man's world

My preoccupation with career choice, clearly, was strongly coupled to my preoccupation with gender and with the choice of a life-partner. (It was a given I would marry and I never questioned it.) In 1949, the biography of Madame Curie *made a very deep impression on me: I want to lead a life like hers,* I wrote. I remember the feeling: I wanted a life working side-by-side with a loving, equal partner. But, oh! The adolescent verbiage: *Pierre Curie writes: "Women of genius are rare." I want to be a woman of genius. I know. I know it too well. But I am just an intelligent kid who spends hours dreaming of being a woman of genius and who does nothing specific to raise her level* … And elsewhere I drool over the descriptions of *those dances* she attended *with the sleighs at night in the open air.* In a more practical vein, I do remember pondering the problem of economic independence and using the young Marie Curie as a model. I thought that with my excellent schooling and knowledge of languages, I could always be, like her, the governess of children in a rich household.

One year later I had decided to study physics and math ('fisico-matemáticas'), which were taught jointly in one single department in the School of Exact Sciences. There was an entrance examination to be taken, and my parents decided I should be coached for it by Manuel Sadosky and Cora Ratto, mathematicians who were making a living through tutoring since they had lost their university professorships. It was the time of Perón's first presidency, and teachers who did not sign an oath of allegiance to the government were summarily dismissed. My father also had been dismissed, but he had an ongoing practice as a lawyer so he was not deprived of a living wage as were the Sadoskys.

Cora Ratto was married to Manuel Sadosky but kept her maiden name. She was a woman of enormous character, a powerful personality. I loved to hear her stories about their student days in France and Italy. During the war years (just a few years before I started going to their apartment for my lessons), Cora had led a strong women's organization that helped the Allied Forces. It was called Junta de la Victoria, and my mother had been a member. They knit socks that were sent to the front, and they also marched in pro-Allies (or anti-Nazi) demonstrations in the streets of Buenos Aires. During one of those demonstrations my mother (a soft, gentle, not-very-politicized soul) ended up in jail (with Cora and other participants). Cora and Manuel were known leftists. To my disbelief, this incident later came to haunt me, seemingly out of nowhere, when I went to the USA embassy to get my entry visa to go to New York to study: The american consul during my interview inquired quite aggressively about my mother's 'communist allegiances.' This was in 1956, the tail end of the McCarthy red-scare era.

I find a few references in my journals to Cora from that year, 1950. I translate: *I went to see Cora Ratto yesterday. "I think it's good that you chose a difficult course of study," she said. That is precisely why I chose it. If already at age 17 I stop using my brain … what can one expect? Effort is good.* And elsewhere: *Cora says that when she and XX* (her woman friend) *find themselves talking about issues regarding household help they stop each other with "Enough! We sound like housewives!"* Cora's daughter, a few years younger than me, is named Corita; she is also a mathematician and has a daughter named Cora Sol. Cora's name is perpetuated, a tribute to her influence on generations of women.

When I was already living in the USA, I read Simone de Beauvoir's book 'The Second Sex' in french. It had been published in 1949 and was virtually unknown in the USA. For an ambitious young woman (which I was), the account of Beauvoir's life with Sartre held enormous fascination. Sartre and his circle were much talked about in Buenos Aires; at home we subscribed to Sartre's journal 'Les Temps Modernes'; the communist-leaning intellectuals who frequented our home had much to say about Sartre's position vis-a-vis Stalin during the war. Simone de Beauvoir described how her book was first conceived, almost by chance. She was considering writing her autobiography and realized that what defined her was the fact that she was a woman. Thus, "wanting to talk about myself, I became aware that to do so I should first have to describe the condition of woman in general." Beauvoir writes, "One is not born, but rather becomes, a woman."

I read the book (borrowed from the O'Donnel branch of the New York Public Library that we frequented) in 1958. I translate my comments: *A genius she isn't (Simone), but undoubtedly she has a good intelligence, culture and dedication to psychological problems; and it's good to feel in agreement with such a person. I am encouraged by the fact that I did not find anything new; it makes me feel I have analyzed my situation correctly. I don't agree with her, however, when she says "… it isn't certain that the world of ideas of women is different from that of men," as Rimbaud says, "since women will find their emancipation when they reach the same situation as men." In short, she advocates Newton's law: same initial conditions, same development. But I don't believe that the initial conditions are* *the same: the structural differences between men and women preclude this and we can only consider initial conditions that are <u>equivalent</u> and lead to development just as broad as that of men, but different. As Beauvoir herself describes, a woman's physical inferiority (i.e. weakness) gives rise to situations that can't be remedied, as far as I can see. . . . Therefore I don't believe in the equality of initial premises. But, like Rimbaud, I do believe that the worlds that women will discover will be different from those of men. However, what, how, or, more to the point, why, is still to be seen; and I would like to see this.*

I find this entry quite interesting, because a big issue that came up 10 years later in the feminist movement was the notion of 'equal opportunity' versus the original rallying cry of 'equality.' And here, in my diary, I find myself pioneering this issue in the terminology of physics.

The feminist movement

In the late 1940s into the 1950s, when I was a young woman in Buenos Aires, women as a group had not developed a consciousness of their shared issues. Each one of us felt as if she was one-of-a-kind, isolated in her problematic. It would be the job of the women's movement to make women aware of their power and the changes that needs must occur in society to grant them their appropriate space, place, and standing. At that time, for example, antibiotics had not yet been discovered (or developed enough); so my perception, say, of giving birth to a child was that the woman ran a big risk in the process. It was also a time when sexual activity and child-bearing were strongly linked, before the development of the diaphragm (let alone the pill, which came much later), the first anti-conception method that put women in charge of the prevention mechanism. These facts strongly colored what it meant to be a woman: sex was a risky proposition. One did not engage in it lightly. The search for an appropriate male partner was all-important. My life in Argentina was drenched with this preoccupation. It was so intense and all-consuming that I find my diaries between ages 13 and 22 almost unbearable to read. (Also many of the entries strike me as repetitious and boring: contemptible because I was so full of myself and so concerned with the impression I made on others, and funny because I was so very naïve.)

When I came to the USA, at age 23, I was married to a classmate who was in every way a partner. The relationship with HRR was in all ways a relationship of equals. We each had a fellowship to study physics at Columbia University in New York, we each had a stipend, we studied together, led a life replete with outings to museums and concerts, had intellectual discussions, shared books and housework. HRR felt very strongly about this lifestyle; inequality within the relationship was never an issue. This was quite uncommon at the time.

When Betty Friedan published her book 'The Feminine Mystique' in 1963, I was already in California, married to GF. Up until this time I had felt that my questions, ruminations, problems about my womanhood, were idiosyncratic, if shared with a few other women. I had no sense that these were societal problems, engendered by the social environment and shared globally by women; the universality of the issues simply had not occurred to me until then. The women's movement grew, and I grew with it. Kate Millet's dictum that 'the personal is political' struck a chord: I had participated in the student movement in Argentina during the embattled years when I was at the university and Perón was president; later I was involved in setting up the first union of professors in California; I valued and admired activism; I supported NOW (the National Organization for Women) with passion.

During that time GF and I constructed our life together. He helped build the physics department and founded the biophysics program at the University of California, San Diego (UCSD). I worked (as researcher and lecturer) at UCSD and then on the faculty at San Diego State University (SDSU, where I stayed until retirement from university life). Raising our two daughters was mostly my responsibility, but I myself had a wife in the person of Genoveva, our mexican housekeeper (who to this day is part of our family) and without whom I could not possibly have done all I did. On the home front much energy went into establishing male-female parity, eliminating gender stereotypes, and overcoming outlooks bred into GF by a male-dominated central-european upbringing. The feminist movement helped create vocabulary that was useful to express ideas that had no name beforehand; for example, 'male chauvinist pig,' or MCP for short. At home it became a term that was bandied about on a daily basis: "Is that MCP behavior?" "You're being an MCP." It was used to judge, to warn, to signal behavior that needed correction. GF resisted, learnt, accepted, and finally laughed and used it freely.

Being in a professional field that is male-dominated

I'm often asked if it wasn't strange to be a woman studying physics. The answer is no, not in Argentina. At the university the number of students was very small, about half were women, and I don't think we contemplated too seriously making a living with the profession. Generally speaking, there was no issue with women choosing what we now call STEM (science, technology, engineering and mathematics) professions. I believe this was because high schools were not co-ed. In a women's-only school, girls were not pitted against boys intellectually at an age when they often act dumb simply because they are so eager to please. This belief of mine is purely anecdotal. At Columbia University, however, the fraction of graduate students in the physics department who were women was about 3 percent: as I remember it, there were 6 of us (Myriam, Noemi, Enid, Lillian, Suzy, and me) and about 200 guys. Three of the women came from latin american countries where the high schools were not coeducational.

On the faculty there were two women; they were not admitted to the Faculty Club because it was 'men only,' so they were unable to, say, have lunch with their colleagues. One of these women was Madame Wu (as everybody called her). She did the crucial experiment in connection with a new law (parity non-conservation) for which the two theorists (C.N. Yang and T.D. Lee) received the 1957 Nobel Prize in Physics; but C.S. Wu was not included. Wu was kind to me and seemed to always acknowledge my presence, whether in class or the Pupin elevator. (Pupin is the name of the physics building and there was a lot of traveling up and down in the elevator.) It went no further than this, but it was good.

At UCSD the physics department was very small when I worked there as a research associate; it was all-male except for myself and faculty member Maria Mayer. When she received the Nobel Prize in 1963, Maria asked me to her office to show me the medal and other Nobel paraphernalia. (I saw this medal again last year in the archives of the UCSD library when I visited in connection with donating GF's papers). In 1964 she came to my party celebrating my PhD — a fun affair with skits and four graduate students wearing mops as wigs, playing and singing Beatles' songs. On one occasion we had dinner at Maria's house, with her husband Joe, and with Hans Jensen, her co-recipient of the Nobel Prize, during one of his visits to La Jolla. For dessert Maria served long-stemmed strawberries to be dipped in whipped cream. (Or was it melted chocolate?) Clearly, they made an impression on me, and long-stemmed strawberries are permanently associated in my mind to the shell model of the nucleus of the atom.

In the natural science department at SDSU I was the only woman on a faculty of about a dozen. My department grouped together scientists from various fields who shared a deep interest in teaching. When I became chair in 1980, I intentionally led the department in hiring another woman. It was funny but touching how the faculty wives rooted for me: "You know how to keep those men in line; good for you!" Although my degree was in physics, I was not a member of the physics department at SDSU, which had no women at all. The old-timers (Garrison and Herschel) invited me a couple of times to physics affairs but it became very clear they only did so because they expected my husband (who was from UCSD, no less, always considered a higher-level institution) to attend. GF was not interested in going. They never invited me again.

Along similar lines: at UCSD there was an indian postdoc who invited us to his house for dinner; this was before we had children. As I remember it, we went, ate, and GF left immediately because he had a poker game — and he was <u>never</u> late for those, God forbid, let alone ever skip one. I had nothing to do for the evening and I sort of suggested I could stay on. But no, he (the postdoc) wasn't interested (there was a wife too, who cooked, but I don't suppose she had a say); clearly it was only important to have the great man there.

This account so far says nothing about my day-to-day interactions with the men. Be they peer students or professors, there are three aspects to mention. First, the oft-repeated comment: "You think like a man." Meant as a compliment, of course. It went together with being accepted and included as 'one of the boys' in a male-dominated field. Second, the special treatment I often received because, let's face it, I was beautiful. One time I was building an amplifier and in the process — soldering and cutting wires and using screwdrivers — I cut myself, prompting my co-worker to say (verbatim): *"Conservation of beauty; it leaves you, and goes into the chassis"* — *a veiled compliment, also, to my soldering capabilities.*[1] The men liked to have me around, and they even said so unabashedly: *"It's a shame you are married, for XX (his boss) and I were thinking it would be very nice to have a nice young single girl working also in this room."* And third, the roughshod treatment I got when a competitive situation arose. When it was time to put in applications for a sabbatical year or for a promotion, and it was known the department could hope to get only one faculty member approved because limited funds were available — that is when my application was passed over, regardless of merit, because, as I was told, "You don't need it: you have a husband to support you."

What is the upshot of all this? On the one hand, that I did not experience as much marginalization and discrimination as many other women did, because I was good-looking. By today's standards, much of what I experienced would be called sexual harassment; but that is not what I felt it to be. In the context of the times, and of my background in latin america, where men routinely pay women compliments, I just took most of it to be expressions of appreciation. In addition, I was

---

[1] 'Conservation laws' are at the very heart of physics; they tell us that nothing disappears, everything is transformed. In the case at hand, my co-worker was saying that I became uglier (less beautiful) by having cut myself, but the amplifier became more beautiful through my soldering work; so the overall beauty of the 'me-and-my-amplifier' system remained constant.

gathered into the fold, at least to the extent that I was not perceived as a threat, as a competitor.

On the other hand, constantly rubbing elbows with men, trying to make it in their world, one ends up acquiring some of those masculine traits linked to aggressiveness. This became apparent to me when, at age 50, I started to work at the Reuben Fleet Science Center in San Diego and my colleagues were mostly women, museum professionals. Not so, I hasten to add, the members of the exhibit development group that I formed and led: these were mostly men — engineers, physicists, and machinists — and I related to them in much the same way as I had with my peers at the university. But outside my own group, I found myself butting heads all too often. Many of the women were not used to frank assessments and critiques of their science exhibits. They took it badly: "Who does she think she is?" Well, <u>she</u> (me) thought she knew her science, and how to present it to non-scientists; she also knew how to argue her points with tough, no-nonsense scientific opponents. But that was not a winning strategy, and eventually I understood I was using an inappropriate approach in this new environment.

Kindred souls

The feminist movement put forth the notion that oftentimes women marry the men they would like to be. I didn't do this. But I remember having fantasized marrying an inordinate number of boys and men, some accessible, others inaccessible and even fictional. I looked through my diaries for evidence of this feminist dictum. What I found were imaginings of what those marriages would be like and, in the case of talented individuals, wishes that I could have such abilities myself. I wanted to play jazz piano like Miguelito, and classical like Daniel; I wanted to ride horses like Ken (in 'My Friend Flicka'), and act like Jean-Louis Barrault and Laurence Olivier. My crushes had to do with my wide-ranging ambitions, but I understood that marriage would not give me the abilities I coveted. At best it would give me proximity, and that was not enough. My fantasies were rooted in my total ignorance of what it meant to be married; perusal of my diaries shows, for example, that my understanding of sex was almost non-existent.

So, what did I want to be? My father put it briefly, *"Querés ser sabia"* — that is, you want to be a sage, a wise one, a 'chacham' as the jews would say. He was right (up to a point). This is why the movie 'Yentl' with Barbra Streisand made a big impression on me. Yentl is a girl in a 'shtetl' (jewish village in Poland or Russia) who wants to study Talmud, just like the boys do. But girls don't study: they marry and toil so their boy-husbands can study. Yentl is bright, so she manages to dress as a boy and gain access to learning. I saw that movie 35 years ago. Recently I read a book on a similar theme, 'The Weight of Ink' by Rachel Kadish. It still reverberates in me. It's about a girl in the 17th century who works for a blind rabbi and uses his identity to have learnèd epistolary conversations with the likes of Spinoza.

Because I am a product of the 20th century I have been granted privileges that my kindred spirits, Yentl and the amanuensis of the blind rabbi, could get only through subterfuge. I have been rewarded with students who could profit from my privilege. A case in point is a young woman who took several semesters of my interactive science class for prospective elementary school teachers. She came to see me at the end of the sequence and informed me she had changed her major: "I found out I love this science stuff and what's more I'm good at it; with you as a role model I figured I don't have to settle for the traditional role of teacher; I can become a professional engineer."

The moral of the story? Being a woman has set the stage for my life to unfold, but it has not clipped my wings.

American

Born and raised in South America, steeped in a very european culture, with many years of living in North America, what do I mean when I say "I am american"? On the one hand, I'm differentiating myself: in spite of a very european upbringing, I feel definitely american. On the other hand, I'm making a statement of inclusion: I'm american, I identify with this whole vast continent, north and south.

American versus european

Buenos Aires is a cosmopolitan city. The immigrant population is large, mostly italian and spanish but with representative communities from most european countries. The original native peoples were not very numerous; so the people you see in the street are mostly caucasian. The design of the city is reminiscent of Paris and Rome: its central park was designed by G.E. Haussman, who also designed Parisian parks and avenues; downtown houses are 'petit hôtels', the avenues are spacious, with trees along the sidewalks, or at least that's the way it was when I was small. When I grew up the culture of the city was decidedly european; music and literature looked towards France, Italy and Spain. In the generation prior to mine, the well-to-do families spent 'the season' (argentinian summer) in Paris, and their children learnt french. The influence of the USA only began to be felt after the second world war.

My brother and I went to british, single-sex schools. (My brother had started in a german school but was quickly removed when Hitler appeared.) Our schools were identical to schools in Britain. The teachers came from Britain; the syllabus was oriented to the graduation exams (called the School Certificate), which were sent to England to be corrected. Our answer sheets were written with carbon paper because, we were told, if the ship carrying them to England was sunk (it was war time when I took the exams), then there would be copies remaining.

My fellow students were mostly from british families: they were the daughters of sheep ranch owners, meat-packing plant administrators (canned corned beef produced in Argentina had a big european market during the war), managers and employees of the railway system. The railroads in Argentina had been built by the british to connect the ranches with the meat-processing plants (british-owned) and the ports of export. British imperialism was strongly felt. In morning assembly at school we sang 'There'll always be an England.' Geography class covered the geography of the British Empire, which was tantamount to the geography of a huge portion of the world: we learnt about the tea plantations in Ceylon, the Brahmaputra river in Burma, the British Protectorate in India, the British Mandate in Palestine.

But these british schools were required to also teach the standard curriculum mandated by the Ministry of Education of Argentina. So, in effect, each school was two schools in one. In the morning all subjects were taught in english and followed an english curriculum (e.g. in math we studied geometry from Euclid's original 'Elements'; history and geography emphasized the British Empire; literature included one Shakespeare play a year). In the afternoon, the spanish curriculum was taught in spanish (with interesting differences, for example, in the way that long division and proportions were handled in math; history, geography, and literature emphasized Spain and its colonies).

In the afternoon, then, it was the remnants of spanish colonialism that were felt. The social sciences dealt in detail with the aztec, maya, and inca civilizations and their conquest; daily life in the viceroyalty of the Rio de la Plata was brought to life. (In a school play, when I was about 9 years old, I played a street seller of candles hawking my wares; or was it a night-watch crying "all is quiet!"?)

There was tension between these two cultures. In the morning at school we behaved according to the british code of fair play; the honor system required honesty, cheating was disgraceful, tell-taling on others was a no-no. In the afternoon you only played straight if you were too dumb to go undetected when you cheated; if you worked and studied it was because you just weren't smart enough to get by relying only on your wits. It is interesting that, whatever split loyalties this educational system may have engendered, forty years later, when Thatcher's England invaded the Falkland islands, there was no question in my mind — and in the minds of many anglo-argentines — that they belonged to Argentina; we were taught that 'las Malvinas son nuestras' (the Malvinas are ours) and this is what we still believed.

Even after I left the british school at age 16, the flavor of life in Buenos Aires was european. Studies in high school and university followed european patterns; textbooks in university were almost exclusively european, mostly french, sometimes italian or english; cultural life in the city was suffused with high-quality theater, music, dance, film, most of it originating in Europe.

My education, then, looked to Europe. It was solid, well rounded and has given me access to some of the finer things in life: a code of honor, foreign languages, social skills, academic knowledge. It has even made traveling the world often feel more homey than foreign: in India the train station buildings and the red cylindrical mailboxes looked just like train stations and mailboxes in the Buenos Aires of my childhood. Yet still, as I grew older in Argentina, my identity remained fiercely rooted in America. The landscapes that moved me were the rolling hills of Córdoba, the lakes and mountains of Patagonia, the vast extensions of fertile pampas traversed by gauchos on horseback at a short gallop. The history that grabbed me were the stories of exploration, circumnavigation of the globe, discovery by the europeans of lands new to them, and the fate of the indigenous people they encountered.

As time went on and I left Argentina to live in the USA, the feelings that rooted me in America remained the same: I loved the huge expanses, a new land with inherent vast possibilities and problematics. Boundlessness. And as I reflect on this I find an account about Alexander von Humboldt that mirrors much of what is in my heart and mind. Three hundred years after the europeans discovered America, Humboldt spent five years exploring central and northern South America. He collected plants and animals, carried out atmospheric and geological measurements, described the geography and native people. The books he published with his reports and observations put the New World on the map; he was "hailed as 'the second Columbus,' 'the scientific discoverer of America'"…who "showed Americans how to imagine themselves as something more than offshoots of European ambition." (The quotes are from Laura Dassaw Walls in 'The Passage to Cosmos.') And that is the essence of it for me: the realization — as a young adult — that americans were beginning to discover themselves and create America's future. And that this creation required both courage and a strong imagination.

American: both north and south

America is vast and unique. Did you ever think about it? It is the only one of the five continents that reaches from one of the Earth's poles to the other. It extends on both sides of the equator, hosts trade winds that blow in different directions in each hemisphere; tornadoes and hurricanes blow counterclockwise in the north, clockwise in the south. In the north you look to the south to see the sun and the moon; in the south you look to the north; the constellations go upside down when you cross over. The continent is so vast that it embraces right-side-up and down-under.

It used to irk me that astronomy books were so chauvinistic, typically describing the skies from the standpoint of an observer in the northern hemisphere. There is, of course, a good reason for that: more people live in the northern than in the southern hemisphere, and (therefore?) the science of astronomy developed in the northern hemisphere. But it seemed to me there should be caveats; people, students, should be made explicitly aware that from the south things look different. Which is why, when I wrote 'Cielito Lindo,'[1] I assumed the viewer was someone in the southern hemisphere, and I purposefully showed the changes experienced as the viewer migrates from south to north.

The sense of belonging to a whole continent manifests itself in my constant mental commute between La Jolla, where I've lived for 60

---

[1] 'Cielito Lindo' Editorial Siglo XXI, 2004; translated at: http://bit.ly/3eWd6sz

years, and Buenos Aires, where I lived my indelible first 25 years. Both of these cities are at latitude 32 degrees. But La Jolla, although it is on the ocean front, is technically a desert, rainfall a few inches a year, green through irrigation. And Buenos Aires, next to the huge Rio de la Plata, is humid: I remember vividly a wall in our dining room where the paint peeled and huge fungi grew immediately after it got wet. The counterpart to this would be the scorpions that every now and then visit our patio in La Jolla.

It is this west coast environment in the USA that I constantly contrast to 'my' Argentina, mostly from Buenos Aires on south. In reality, this mental commute maps the dorsal spine of the continent, the mountain chain that spans it from north to south, the Sierra Nevada that morphs into the Andes. The longest mountain chain in the world. Up and down it I go in my mind, in my imagination. And I ponder. I ponder the geography and the history: the huge lands inhabited by native people; the expansion movements, to the west in the USA, to the south in Argentina.

My musings in this write-up are purely about the land. The lyrics of 'This land is your land' never fail to make me shiver with emotion:

> This land is your land, this land is my land
> From California, to the New York island
> From the Redwood Forest, to the Gulf Stream waters
> This land was made for you and me

But I want to add another verse, something like this:

> This land is your land, this land is my land
> From the Altiplano, to the humid Pampa
> From the torrid jungles, to Patagonia's ice-cap
> This land was made for you and me

The american expansion to the west, in the north. In 1804, commissioned by president Jefferson to find a passage across the USA to the Pacific ocean, Lewis and Clark sailed up the Missouri river. They surveyed and mapped their journey, from the Mississippi river, up the Missouri river through Montana state, across the continental divide on the Rockies, and on to the western side, down the Snake river to the Columbia river, to the Pacific ocean in Oregon state.

Most of this land, of course, was already occupied by native americans — the shoshone, the chinook, the sioux. This area is personally meaningful to me because it is where Paoli (our younger daughter) lives. Twenty-five years ago she chose to do her graduate studies in Bozeman, Montana. (Visualize it on the map: an hour away from Yellowstone National Park.) Addicted to the mountains, as she was and remains, she has lived there ever since. Her partner JoJo is Montana born and bred. His family's mountain cabin is on what used to be crow indian reservation land (and was probably unfairly taken).

Later in the 1800s, John Wesley ('Wes') Powell, one-armed (as a result of the civil war) and full of ideas and energy, continued the exploration of the west by going south, down the Colorado river. The story is magnificently told in 'Beyond the 100th Meridian' by W. Stegner. What is remarkable about his adventure is that it was driven by the conviction that the 'Great American Desert' — just east of the Rocky Mountains — was habitable. Through irrigation, he postulated, the parched plains on the east slope of the Rockies, the desert, could become a 'Garden.' This meant that fundamental changes would need to be made in the way land was allocated. He showed that detailed, scientific surveys were essential to determine the location of water sources relative to land holdings. The ensuing regulations for apportioning land and irrigation resources caused much political upheaval, but Powell's quest did, ultimately, result in the creation of national institutions of fundamental importance, such as the US Geological Survey. In the final years of his career, Powell shifted from geological to anthropological pursuits, based in the Bureau of American Ethnology that he had founded, prompted by his early fascination with the native peoples he encountered on his journeys.

Why is this part of the frontier story especially interesting to me? Those of us who live in the California desert know what it means to be 'water-challenged.' It brings to mind an israeli film which dealt with the rescue operation Solomon, that brought hundreds of ethiopian jews to the promised land. There is a scene in which a young ethiopian boy is taking a shower just after arrival in Israel, and, horrified at seeing the water run into the drainage, he stoops and tries to collect it with his hands. We, in California, are not water-deprived but are, yes, water-conscious. Driving along the eastern slope of the Sierras when we go to (and come from) hiking and skiing expeditions, I don't cease to be reminded of the water wars — described by Marc Reisner in his book 'Cadillac Desert' — when the once-pastoral landscape of the Owens Valley was dried out in order to get running water to the residents of Los Angeles. A story of water-control runs along the borders of my life: from the Aswan dam that got my egyptologist father (and me) to Sudan in the 1960s, to the Hoover Dam (now crowned with one of the british bridges that used to service the river Thames) where we rowed and floated our canoes with my elder daughter Shoshanah's Girl Scout troop in the 1980s.

The american expansion further south, in the south. I was shocked when I first came across the notion of 'manifest destiny,' a term coined in the mid-1800s: the ideology that the expansion of white USA to the west, across the continent, was both justified and inevitable; indeed, it was religiously ordained, no less. I had been brought up with the knowledge that the spaniards had killed the aztecs, maya, and inca for their silver and gold, and that they sent jesuit missionaries to convert them to christianity. But killing them for their land? Of course, that is precisely what was happening in the nascent Argentina of the 1800s. These were not the conquistadores of the 1500s. As in the USA, these were the settlers themselves, those who had recently won their independence from colonial powers, now asserting their own form of imperialism.

In the 1830s, just about the time when Darwin was sailing the Beagle down Argentina's coast, Juan Manuel Rosas was governing the land. Rosas, heeding the demand of his fellow landowners in the province of Buenos Aires, organized the first campaign in what later became 'the conquest of the desert.' The purpose was to stop the incursions of the indigenous people into the ranches to steal cattle. A great native chief called Calfucurá arose in these times, and a détente with the white landowners was reached for many years. His remains ended up in the Natural History Museum of La Plata, and only last year they were returned to the mapuche community for proper burial. I have a sense of personal connection with these events because the years the mapuches started to demand restitution of their peoples' human remains coincided with the years I worked at that museum (developing the Egyptian Hall). I remember the comings and goings of the mapuche leaders and the reconstruction of the exhibit halls when the remains were removed.

Towards the end of the 1800s, general Julio Roca (so well rendered in 'Soy Roca' by Felix Luna) led a campaign to make the final push south and establish boundaries between argentinian and indian territory. This campaign proposed peopling the 'desert' — referring to the land to the south as if it were uninhabited. It became outright war; the natives were decimated. Roca, riding on his success, was elected president of the Republic.

There is a statue of Julio A. Roca, the general of this genocide, that I passed every day when I attended the University of Buenos Aires. In recent years it has been smeared with red paint by activists. I find myself approving the red smear: it's better than taking the statue down; it's adding a present-day reflection, saying times have been a-changing and this man is not a hero after all.

June 2020. With designer Leandro Panetta we are currently deep into the conceptualization of content for a Visitor Complex being developed in Patagonia, latitude 49 degrees. This is land where for thousands of years the tehuelche natives roamed, hunting guanacos for their pelts and meat. Huemul (deer) roamed and pumas (mountain lions) preyed. Today, the tehuelches have disappeared and the animal species are much diminished. Our visitor center, sponsored by the Tompkins Conservation Foundation, will highlight the rewilding efforts in the area. These will bring back many species, though not the tehuelches. It is, however, an attempt to spread balm over a much-scarred land, and I'm pleased to be a part of this new project.

The constant north-south commute. Nowadays Buenos Aires tends to be noisy, often dirty; transactions are difficult; daily life complicated. But there is a latin, mediterranean quality to life in the cafés, the interaction with people, the love of good food, of a good schmooze. Back in La Jolla life is orderly, simple; everything seems sanitized, even human relations. Spend half a year in one place, you yearn for the other. In Argentina, after several weeks, I understand why I had to come and live in the USA to get anything accomplished. In the States, after some time, I miss the chaotic warmth of argentinian society.

As GF and I used to say — when we did our yearly orthogonal trips, he to the east (Israel), me to the south (Argentina) — the only place one is really totally content is in the airplane, coming and going...

1997 Golo 'n' Drina

Draft of a flip-book, based on the story of the swallows of San Juan Capistrano in California, with instructions for assembly

Background

Swallow in spanish is Golondrina. Hence, Golo 'n' Drina.

The story is a metaphor of my own life: the yearly trip to Argentina to get new, strong feathers that will last another year; the nest building, giving birth to the young, in Southern California; the North-South-North-South repetitive voyages, over sundry cultures and awesome sights.

Instructions for assembly and viewing as a flip-book

1. Cut out the 3 strips from each page along the full horizontal lines. (Alternatively, you may want to photocopy the pages onto thicker paper and cut the strips from the copies.) You will end up with 27 strips (numbered from 0 to 26).

2. Fold each strip along the dashed vertical line in the center, with the printed content inside. As you do so, lay the folded strips, with their **open sides at the left,** in order, one on top of the next. You will have a stack of 27 folded strips, with strip 0 on the bottom of the stack and strip 26 on the top.

3. Attach the folded strips in order: you are gluing or double sticky-taping the blank sides together (attaching just the edges is enough).

4. Staple or otherwise bind the folded edges together to create the completed booklet. Or you can use a paper clamp for the binding.

5. Flip the pages of the booklet by holding the bound edge of the flip-book in your left hand, putting the thumb of your right hand on the right edge of the book, and moving your thumb slowly and smoothly away from you to let the pages flip one by one from front to back. You'll see the swallow appear in the upper right corner, flying first North and then back to the South.

Flip-book animation

0A

0B

1A

1B

2A

2B

32

3A

One afternoon in February
they take off from
the plaza in Goya
along the river Paraná.
Thousands of birds

3B

4

starting together on a trip
Pole. They fly
past the huge Iguazú
waterfalls,
into the Swamplands

halfway to the North

of Brazil.

5

the animals of the
watch them go by:

the capybara

the anaconda

Swamplands

the yacaré

the piranha

34

6

Still North they fly, over the great rivers, the Amazon and the Orinoco.

7

past Angel Falls, the world's tallest waterfall;

8

the mountains are and the insects are

always keeping their distance from the

snow-capped Andes where too high-- too cold, too bare- too few.

9 the swallows feed on
they swoop
to catch and
eat them

insects:

on the wing

10
For twenty days
now
they've been
stopping
only to sleep at night

For twenty days
now

they've been
flying

all day long.

11 Below them are the
pyramids built by the
Mayas one thousand
years ago.

12.

And the whales, also going North flutting along the coast of California with their newborns.

13

In March, one month after starting their trip, the swallows arrive in San Juan Capistrano, the place where Drina was born.

14 The older swallows go to live in their old nests.

But Drina is young, not yet one year old. She doesn't have a nest. She has to build her own.

15. Nearby, a te-swallow He calls out to Drina.

has started a nest.

She picks up mud from a puddle and joins him.

16 Mud pellet by mud

pellet they build their nest.

17 On the dry grass inside the finished nest Drina lays four eggs.

Two weeks later they hatch.

THE WARP

18   By June the young swallows fly as well as their mother.

19
Then one day in September Drina smells Winter in the air. It will soon be cold in San Juan Capistrano.

It is time to leave for Goya, where Summer is about to start.

20   Drina and her family will fly half way to the South Pole past the pyramids,

21 the great rivers,

22 the animals of the swamplands,

23 the wide waterfalls,

24   to Gaya,
where they will live
by the river Paraná
and change their
feathers.

25   Until the days
turn short and cold
again,
And the time comes
to fly North again.

26   So that wherever
the Swallow is,
you can be
pretty sure
it is Summer.

48

The intellect; the rational mind

April 1951. I'm 18 years old. I translate: *I'm very unhappy that I didn't better use the month of March. Very unhappy. As usual, when the working year starts I'll be sorry; ah! I didn't read the Greeks during vacation when I had time; ah! I didn't learn how to sew; ah! I didn't study art history; ah! I didn't start on mathematical analysis. It drives me crazy that I don't better use my precious time. During vacation when I'm really resting it doesn't matter, but here in BsAs it really bothers me.*

A week ago, when I was in the midst of such reflections about the scarcity of time when there's so much to learn (when I think about it I'm horrified), H (my brother) interrupts me with: "You are like Kant, you think that the only link between man and the world is through knowledge." He really surprised me because yes, that's what I thought (although I didn't have the foggiest idea that Kant thought likewise) without knowing it in words (explicitly). However, that conviction, that I held for the past two years, was falling apart this last week. Well, not falling apart but attenuating. I was finding another link I had never before wanted to recognize: experience.... Although I had heard it expressed frequently at home, by my father, I never quite understood.

Here the diary goes into some considerations about Hermann Hesse and the Steppenwolf. *This is one more step in growing up. Incredible how one evolves. But I insist that when there is no way to get experience, the center of our activities must be study to increase knowledge. Which is why I am still bothered by time that is really just frittered away. I have something else to say: the other day I was thinking that I, who feel so comfortable in a musical or sporty environment and will feel comfortable in a mathematical-scientific environment, would be a non-entity among lawyers or artists.*

In trying to find a way into this strand of my warp, the one that deals with my way of thinking, I find those last few lines from my journal quote to be of interest: at age 18 I may not have known what I was going to do with my life, but I did know I was not 'comfortable,' that is, interested, in law or, for that matter, in business, finances, or painting. So, what was it that drove me toward science? What other possibilities did I discard along the way? This exploration is meaningful because, although I did become a physicist, in answering questions about my identity I would not define myself as a scientist. The defining trait, rather, is a characteristic of mind, a particular way of thinking; while it underlies my choice of profession, it underlies much more as well.

Choosing science. In Argentina, when you finished high school — a very european-style, well-rounded course of study in my day — you immediately chose a profession and went straight into that discipline: medicine, philosophy, literature, history, engineering, mathematics, physics, architecture… I had loved anatomy and physiology in high school and thought medicine might be an interesting career. One of my boyfriends at the time — a peruvian fellow who, like so many other latin americans at the time, had come to Buenos Aires to become a doctor — took me to the university amphitheater to observe an operation. It was a child with encephalitis; the skull was so soft that the surgeon cut it open with scissors to let out the liquid. I loved it. But during some other site visit to one of the municipal hospitals it occurred to me that many of the people there were being cured of ills that could have been avoided. A case in point: a child with bad burns due to hot oil spilling on him because he brushed against the handle of a frying pan that was on the stove; his harried mother had left the handle sticking out; surely this could have been prevented with appropriate social services? Most issues seemed to be political or educational or psychological rather than purely medical. I could not see myself curing these kinds of ills, socially provoked. In hindsight, I did not even consider working on the root cause of physical disease. The labs of Houssay and Leloir were functioning then; but this avenue never crossed my mind. I only considered clinical work, the kind my uncle and cousin did.

In school I had also liked geometry, algebra, and logic; I had a penchant for philosophical questions about knowing. What I really enjoyed most, however, were languages: their structure, syntax, etymologies and rhythms, rhymes, alliterations, and poetry. I thought comparative literature would be a wonderful field of study. But I also thought it could be done on the side, as an avocation. Math and the sciences, on the other hand, required a discipline of thought that could only be learnt with proper teaching.[1] Add to this the argument that literature did not seem to have practical value, societal value. *May 1955: I think I would be ashamed to earn my living as a film star or by producing 'beautiful things' such as a novel. It seems illogical that society would pay for something that is not of immediate use, something practical.* Thus, the stage was set for my choosing to study mathematical physics.

I was going for the queen of sciences, arguably physics at the time. I remember a heated afternoon discussion with a woman friend who studied chemistry and claimed <u>it</u> was the queen of sciences. But I held my ground and invoked the philosophical dimensions of quantum physics and the mathematics strung along with it. (I had the delta function and the theory of distributions in mind). Those were heady days. We studied quantum mechanics from the book by Dirac with his bras and kets (brackets). I read Reichenbach and delved into positivism and idealism. David Bohm held our attention. If you thought thinking was important, then these were the things to think about.

A program I saw recently on television celebrating the 100-year anniversary of Einstein's theory of relativity makes me comment on the impact this subject matter had on us at the time. We studied it, of course: special relativity and tensor analysis to go with general relativity. But Einstein's gravity was not the paradigm people were working on then. The paradigm, at the time I was a student, was quantum theory and its interpretation; quantum mechanics was already in the classroom; quantum electrodynamics was the research field of the day, waiting

---

[1] I have found the identical argument put forth by Brenda Milner in her autobiography written for the Journal of Neurophysiology.

for a breakthrough that was in gestation.[2] Einstein, however, was very much an icon, and I remember clearly going to the telephone when my fellow student Lucia Lagatta called me (from a public phone, since they had no phone line in her house) to announce: "Se nos murió el viejito" which I translate as "Our old man has died" — but this doesn't nearly capture the pathos…

Our cohort was small: four girls and four boys, give or take. But many of our courses had large classes because they were taken together with students from engineering. The mathematics department was well staffed with excellent professors; physics had very few teachers — it was an embryonic field, mostly theoretical, as is characteristic of countries with few resources. Many of the better minds and teachers were not to be found at the university, for the Perón government, in power at the time, demanded an oath of allegiance these professors had been unwilling to sign. This was also the time of the Richter affair, when Argentina claimed to have the atomic bomb. The dismantling of this lie gave rise to a wonderful school of physics in the lake region (Bariloche), where I attended my (and its) first summer school.

During these years I met and married fellow student HRR. Together we embarked on the quest for fellowships to do graduate studies at a good physics school abroad. HRR, ever resourceful, found out there were fellowships given by UNESCO to Argentina that no one seemed to know about and were going unused. The agency for obtaining them was the Department of Foreign Affairs (Ministerio de Relaciones Exteriores). As is usual — at least in latin american countries — both the representative to UNESCO (Eduardo Mallea) and the Minister of Foreign Affairs (Mujica Láinez) were well-known writers. Another well-known writer who knew them both was family friend Jorge Luis Borges. At the time Borges was director of the national library, where we went to see him to ask for letters of recommendation. We got the letters and the fellowships and ended up at Columbia University in New York City in the physics department.

---

[2] We learnt about Feynman diagrams from student friends who were in Brazil doing their theses at the time Feynman was there; Feynman, Schwinger and Tomonaga received the 1965 Nobel Prize for developing QED (Quantum Electro-Dynamcs).

The physics department at Columbia was very high-powered. A ground-breaking discovery had just been made — we read about it on the airplane going to New York from Buenos Aires — which resulted in T.D. Lee and C.N. Yang getting the Nobel Prize that very year (1957). One of our first-semester courses (statistical mechanics) was with T.D. Lee. Another of our courses (nuclear physics) was with C.S. Wu (known to us as Madame Wu) who didn't get the Nobel Prize with him, but should have. Other professors of ours received Nobel Prizes later on (C.H. Townes in 1964; J. Steinberger and L. Lederman in 1983). The student body was inordinately competitive. I'd never seen anything like it before.

Always aiming for the stars and getting myself into untenable situations, I tried to be a thesis student of T.D. Lee's. Thinking back, I had no idea what I was doing: I was trying to play totally out of my league. It became clear that I needed to do an experimental thesis — not a theoretical one. This needs some clarification. A theorist invents explanations for the way the physical world behaves. A good theorist — like T.D. Lee, like Einstein or F. Dyson or Feynman — is worth his/her weight in gold. A bad theorist is worthless. Experimentalists can also be good or bad; but at least they work with the real world of matter and not with ideas manufactured in their heads. So there is usually the chance they will discover something of interest about the way the universe behaves. Therefore, if my chances of being a good theoretician were meager, it was better I join the ranks of experimentalists doing solid, pragmatic work. And this is how I ended up working for Charlie Townes.

Townes had a large group — he was doing his maser stuff and was inventing the laser and needed to find good masing/lasing materials. I found a niche there, growing crystals and studying electron-spin relaxation times. Then Townes left New York to become scientific advisor to Eisenhower (the US president) in Washington DC. And he needed colleagues to come to Columbia University and take care of his graduate students. So that is how GF became a visiting professor at Columbia University, taught a course in solid state physics, and got me as a graduate student.

Scientific thinking as a way of being. GF and I met over those crystals I tried to grow, but we had arrived at crystals through very different roads. I have recounted how I began with math and philosophy. Then I realized that philosophical problems end up being solved by physicists. The philosophers pose the problem (is matter discrete or continuous? do we move around the Sun or does the Sun revolve around the Earth?) but in the end, given several theories to explain a physical phenomenon, it is observation and experiment that decide the issue. So that was my road to physics, and it's how I ended up with the crystals. And GF? He was a tinkerer. He was blowing up his mother's bathtub with the sodium in his chemistry set. He was making crystal radios to talk to his childhood friend Tommy Hornak (who'd be a Hewlett Packard top engineer years later). He was cutting the feedback loop in radios of arab customers in Haifa (who wanted their radios to blare uninhibited) in order to make money to come to the USA to study. And when he did get here he went to Berkeley and graduated in electrical engineering. But that led to experimental physics, because GF was really into understanding things at a fundamental level. As was I. He, having come a ways from his early tinkering days. Me, having come a ways from my early philosophical days.

I learnt so much from him. How to think in tangible, practical, disciplined ways. How to problem-solve step by step. Of course, I learnt it because I was ready, and open to his way of thinking; it grabbed me; it appealed to the way I wanted to be — to understand and act — in the world. And he, in turn, learnt not to say with a sardonic sneer: "How would I know: am I a philosopher?" Which enraged me because, after all, in his fashion, he <u>was</u> (a philosopher).

One upshot of all this was that we developed a common language of scientific similes and metaphors. It was both a shortcut and a rich conceptual basis for everyday conversation. One example from my diary of 1968: *June 11. Went to the baccalaureate of Radcliffe at the Memorial Chapel at Harvard. George Wald spoke. He used a kind of scientific historical theme, telling how stars are formed, and how atoms are formed from dying stars, and then molecules and man. How, therefore, man is a bit of a star. And, also, how to the religious saying that "we are children of God" one can parallel "we are children of the Universe;" that, if there is not another life in Heaven, we can be certain that if this life ceases, there is or will be another life someplace else, sometime else.* And here there is an addition of mine in the margin, clearly after I told all this to GF: *As Gy said, the idea of a canonical ensemble; the probability of something happening in a system sometime is the same as that of something happening in one of a whole set or ensemble of identical systems at anytime. Substitute time for place.* The entry goes on, about the address: *It was OK for the kind of thing it was. I found it very passé and not even stirring.*

Now that GF is gone I find I miss our way of communicating more than I can express. It gave sparkle and depth to verbal exchange. A shared language, much like what I imagine identical twins sometimes develop; it came from having lived in the same 'soup' and having sought an underlying rational framework for understanding and communicating. 'Being on the same wavelength' doesn't begin to capture it, but it's a start.

Playfulness and urgency. The year GF and I spent in Boston (1967–68), I became involved in the Elementary Science Study (ESS) program of the post-Sputnik explosion in science education (what would now be called STEM: the acronym for programs in science, technology, engineering, and mathematics). I loved all aspects of the ESS program; I lapped it up. I remember saying: "If I had been taught science like this, I would not have needed to go into physics." An exaggeration of course, but the meaning was that I went into physics because I needed to learn the scientific way of thinking in order to know how to approach problems and understand the world around us. The hands-on, phenomenon-based approach to science learning offered by the ESS units made the student think in the way I had wanted to think but didn't know how. And if I'd learnt it from an early age I wouldn't have needed the university to teach me, and I could have done literature happily.

In writing this, I find it interesting that the terms 'curiosity' and 'inquisitiveness'— that appear so often when talking about this kind of science teaching and learning — don't seem to come up in my attempts to describe what drove me. It is their absence as explicit terms that I find odd. For, after all, it is never-ending curiosity that drives the quest for knowledge, and I know I have plenty of that. I think perhaps my quest was always a little dogged, determined, insatiable; it lacked a certain playfulness, a ludic component that I've always emphasized in the science museum and the classroom. Perhaps it has to do with a pervasive sense of urgency as I describe in my diary entry at the beginning of this chapter. GF also had a sense of running time, a feeling that every minute was precious, not to be squandered. My father had a pocket watch on a gold chain that he put on the podium to track time when he lectured. My children and grandchildren have smart cell phones that are tied in to a time-telling device. But in my generation, we had wristwatches. GF checked his constantly; it was almost a tic (or a toc?). Shoshanah, our daughter, now that he's gone, loves to wear the watch that didn't need to be wound up, because GF's own pulse kept it going.

Association, synthesis, and aesthetics. Ultimately, it turns out that science does not have that big a role in what I've called the intellect, the rational mind. Science is the field in which I learnt to think like I do. Call it rational; call it logical. Ultimately, what I most cherish is the use of two skills: association and synthesis.

My father, a historian and jurist, used associative thinking constantly: "Everything I know," he used to tell me, "acts like a hitching post for anchoring new knowledge." My mother would say, with overt admiration, "I don't know how you remember all that!" And he responded "I have landmarks in my mind; I tie things in to existing landmarks." As do I, his daughter.

As to my synthetic bent, it is manifest in these writings. I have a hard time expounding, explaining, amplifying, even analyzing. It is the synthesis I go for, the bringing together, the compact summarizing. That is why I love writing the captions to exhibits: the essence of what is being shown needs to be expressed in a minimal amount of space. Just my cup of tea. This is also why my favorite piece of work is what I've done on symmetry, both the book[3] and the interactive exhibition.[4] (I was captivated with symmetry early on: when I started to work on

---

[3] Simetría, 2009, Editorial Siglo XXI

[4] Symmetry, 1991, Reuben H. Fleet Science Center, San Diego, California

crystals in 1959 I gave a set of talks on group theory — the theory underlying symmetries — during the friday seminars of Townes' group at Columbia University).

Synthetic thought is accompanied by a particular aesthetics. It's an aesthetics of simple, congruent design — I would not call it minimalist. The house I was born in, my parents' home, was built in Bauhaus style. The architect who designed it (A. Vilar) told my mother that he would choose (some of) the furniture (as Bauhaus design required). So, in 1932, our Buenos Aires house had Breuer chairs. Of course, I was not born yet when the house was built. But its style underscores my mental framework and I find it (the style) immensely comforting.

And this is as close as I can come to deciphering my mind.

Jewish

Argentinian jew

I was born and raised in Argentina. So were my parents. And my mother's parents too. The grandparents on my paternal side and the great-grandparents on my maternal side are from Russia, Belorussia and Besarabia respectively. The area known as the Pale of Settlement. I think of it as the mesopotamia in between the Dniester and the Dnieper rivers, the place where most jews seem to come from that I meet and befriend. They are all over in the diaspora, yet they all came from towns just a few hundred kilometers removed from one another along the Dniester.

Jews whose roots in Argentina go back to the 1800s are, by and large, part of the Barón Hirsch movement. The Barón Hirsch was a jewish frenchman who went to Russia to sell trains to the czar and, seeing the dreadful living conditions of his fellow jews, came up with schemes to better their circumstances in Russia. When these failed, he forged a plan to help the jews leave Russia. His friends at the argentinian embassy in Paris told him that Argentina needed immigrants and explicitly welcomed jews. The Barón established the Jewish Colonization Agency to manage his project, bought land in Argentina (also in southern Brazil) and, within 6 months in 1881, ships sailing from Bremen and Le Havre carried 2,500 russian jews to become farmers in the new colonies. Most of these jews would have preferred to go to Palestine. But the Ottoman Empire ruled there and did not want the jews. (Just as the british did not want them during the second world war 50 years later).

Depending on one's point of view, the Barón Hirsch Jewish Colonies project was a total failure or a great success. From the standpoint of the establishment of an ongoing agricultural settlement of 3 million people, as originally envisaged, the project was a dismal failure. The population of the colonies barely reached 26,000 by the time of the first world war. These days there are only vestiges left of the original settlements: a few of the farms owned by absentee landlords and worked by non-Jews; here and there, a synagogue that seldom collects a minyan;[1] lost in the fields, a cemetery…

But the failure of the agricultural project was due to the enormous success of the jews themselves in the new country. The very first generation of children born in Argentina — among them my father and uncle and, on my mother's side, my great uncles and aunts — left the countryside to study in the big cities, and became successful professionals and business people. They made up the country's middle class and intelligentsia and by the time the next generation was born, these russian jews from the colonies were taking up important positions in Argentina's government, universities, and commerce. Careers could be vertiginous: my father — who went to elementary school riding bareback on the same horse as his two brothers closest in age — became a professor at the University of Buenos Aires and a member of the National Academy of Letters (where, as different from, say, the prestigious National Academy of Sciences in the USA, the number of members is limited to 24, so a new appointment is made only when an academician dies and leaves a spot open).

All this to say that to be an argentinian jew who traces her lineage to the 'colonias' has special meaning to those in the know. The phrase 'es paisano de las colonias' (he is a fellow countryman from the colonies) rules out the german and other european jews who came escaping Hitler's rise to power; it also rules out the polish and other european jews who had come earlier to the cities and were never farmers of argentinian soil. A paisano de las colonias had to ride horses, co-live with the gauchos, and in fact, become a 'gaucho judío.' He had to learn how to make a living from the soil. He had to contend with the local agents of the colonization project. A paisano de las colonias, somehow, is more argentinian than other jews.

---

[1] Ritual minimum number of devotees needed to conduct a service.

So far I've talked about my jewish roots, my provenance. But if my culture and values are jewish, as far as beliefs go I'm agnostic. My father was agnostic, as were so many intellectuals of his generation. Part of this stance stems from a rational view of the universe and society, a Spinoza-like worldview. Part of it is a reaction to religion entrenched in government: christianity in Argentina and the USA, orthodox judaism in Israel, not to mention radical Islam. To my auto-definition, then, I would add 'agnostic': agnostic argentinian jew.

My jewish identity expands in the USA

Coming to the USA provided another layer to my jewish background. When I arrived in New York I remember looking at the windows of high-rise apartments during Passover and seeing families at the dinner table with lit candles, the men wearing kippahs. I couldn't believe the number of families who were celebrating the holiday, going through the ritual. In Buenos Aires I had only ever attended one passover seder. My only contact with the synagogue was on the high holidays when I went with my mother to greet her mother, who did attend services. This grandmother (the only grandparent I ever knew) had her festive dinners at the house of her brothers.

As I learnt over the years, in the USA it's important to have a religious identity. Belonging to a religious community provides socialization and a sense of belonging. These are otherwise hard to come by in a society where people are constantly on the move following jobs, so that families and friends end up dispersed. In Buenos Aires, where there is less mobility, the family and the neighborhood provide the cocoon, the containment needed to keep alienation at bay.

In San Diego, we belonged to a temple for a few years only, while our elder daughter Shoshanah became a bat mitzvah. She requested this ceremonial passage to adulthood to be in syntony with the other jewish girls in her class. To this day Shoshanah and her family belong to a congregation and, indeed, much of their social life is linked to this group. Our younger daughter Paoli, on the other hand, was not interested in becoming a bat mitzvah. But (as an adult) she went to live in Montana, far from us, and she now does occasionally participate in the rituals and get-togethers of a congregation in her town. Both our daughters were born and raised in the USA, and they follow the mores of their country. GF and I as immigrants (this always sounds funny to me), with very different prior experiences from our daughters', did not seek a formal connection to religion. One might say the scientific community satisfied our needs.

When we arrived in La Jolla, we were invited to Passover seder by academic colleagues. This was meaningful to GF, whose family had celebrated the jewish holidays in Czechoslovakia. I said to GF: "I will go with you, but if you want to do a seder at home it will be over my dead body." When Shoshanah was two we were coming home from one of these celebrations; she was standing on the front seat of our open convertible (this was before seat belts and children's car seats) belting out "Dai dai yenu, dai dai yenu, daiyenu daiyenú." Such joy! The next year, when Paoli was born, I was hosting our first seder at home. How could I deny our children the pleasure of singing all those songs, preparing all that special food, telling stories at the table, hunting for the afikomen with the other children?! For fifteen years we alternated houses for the seder with Shelly Schultz and his family.[2] The grandparents of Shelly's family used to come from New York and participate. Now that Shelly and GF are no longer alive, the children (ours and theirs) have started alternating the seders, with their own children participating.

...and it expands further through connection with Israel

The connection I made with Israel via GF (who lived there from 1941–1946) has given me a belated sense of prideful belonging to the jewish world. When the State of Israel was created I was still in Buenos Aires: everybody celebrated; my parents held a party. But I did not grasp the meaning, the hugeness of what had happened. I began to understand when GF and I first went to Israel, a few months after we got married, to visit GF's parents, and his sister Erika with her four children. We also visited — as we did every single trip of the very many we took to

---

2 Shelly Schultz and I were graduate students together at Columbia University; he came to UCSD in 1960 as a member of GF's physics group.

Israel — a few of GF's friends from Slovakia who had also found refuge in Palestine (the british mandate that later became Israel). GF was sixteen years old when he escaped from German-occupied Slovakia with a small cohort from the Shomer Ha Zair (a leftist movement) and made it to Palestine. His sister was already there, having arrived earlier through a different escape route. His parents arrived in Israel after the war (which they spent in hiding in Slovakia). GF spent the first few years at kibbutz Merchavia, then in Haifa, before coming to the USA to study — and, as it turned out, to stay, although that was not the original plan. His feelings about Israel were very strong and always remained so, in spite of his disappointment with the political scene in recent times.

I, too, have come to love Israel. The politics don't enter into these feelings, just like the sometimes-terrible politics in Argentina do not diminish my love for the country. I love Israel's history, ancient and modern. I love Jerusalem. I love the hebrew language — its logical structure. I also love the fact that the hebrew spoken on the street is similar to biblical hebrew, the same as in the 'Tanakh' (the Jewish Bible or Old Testament).

As I was writing this, an anecdote came to mind: when GF first saw me, playing tennis at a physics conference in the Catskills, he said (so he tells me) to his colleague and friend standing next to him: "That is the girl I'm going to marry." It turned out he thought I was israeli because I wore no lipstick, no make-up (a rare thing in the USA in the fifties). By the time he found out I was not israeli — it was too late.

So I guess the conclusion is that this american jew, daughter of a gaucho judío, has acquired israeli trappings over the years — and remains an agnostic.

1995 The Colonias

First chapter for a biography of my father,
with endnotes (a – k) originally provided for close family

I've decided to call him Abi, although for me he was always "papi". But in a long narrative like this one, "papi" lends itself to misinterpretations; and Abi is what his elder grandchildren called him: Abi for "abuelo", of course, but also for "Abraham". So it is Abi that this story will be about.

Abi died in the year 1983. He was 85 (or was it 87?) years old[1]. In his latter years, aware of how little we, his children, knew about his early life, I tried to steer the conversations with him to those days. Because Abi talked very little about his childhood. We knew he had been born and raised in the pampas, near Carlos Casares in the province of Buenos Aires, in one of the Jewish colonies of Baron Hirsch. Visible remainders of this were his skill in horseback riding, the bombachas (gaucho-style pants), alpargatas (rope-soled canvas footwear) and boina (beret) that he wore, and the mate amargo that he drank.[2]

He had been very close to his mother. He remembered helping her prepare the challah (plaited bread) on Fridays and baking it in the mud oven. He also told how, when he was a student in Buenos Aires, he could only help his mother with the few pesos he earned as prefect (senior student preserver-of-order-in-the-classroom) in high school.

---

[1] Abi was born in Colonia Mauricio on July 7, 1898, although in his official documents the recorded date is June 20, 1896. He explained that his birth date was purposely misreported so he could begin school sooner.

[2] It seems these leftover habits from their days in the countryside gave rise to their use of the term "paisano". Etymologically, a paisano is someone from the same country as the speaker, but in South America the term means peasant or countryside dweller. Abi would say "They are paisanos" when talking about fellow Jews.

Eventually, when Abi and his brother Jacobo (who became a well-known gynecologist, professor at the University of Buenos Aires) achieved good economic standing, they brought their parents to live in Buenos Aires. But I did not know much more.

So it was that during my summer visits, we chatted in the garden of the house that we both loved so much in Arribeños (in the neighborhood of Belgrano de las Barrancas), as he sipped mate while I pruned the vines. We joked that not everyone has the luxury of importing a gardener from the United States (where I live) to cut back the ivy. It was during these summer gardening sessions that I found out what follows, told more or less in Abi's own words.

1. Childhood memories: Colonia Mauricio and the family

Abi's father, Salomón Rosenvasser, was called Roitman in Russia. Eliezer Shloimo Roitman. Name changes were common in the Jewish community. For example, a requisite for going to the Baron Hirsch colonies was having sons (who could help with the work in the fields). So many a young man ended up with a new name as he went "on loan" to a family that had only daughters or to a childless couple. Sons were also exchanged during the time of the czars in order to avoid military service — which was tremendously long (twenty-five years!) and from which only sons of widowed mothers were exempt. Childless widows, then, "adopted" a son in order to save him from the military service.

According to Abi, the name Roitman was changed at the time of obtaining the passports. Who knows why. The fact is that when the family entered Argentina it was registered in the port of Buenos Aires as Rhozenvvhasir. Thank goodness we did not keep that spelling! Don Salomón got rid of the h's and the z and the double v, so we are not even rosewater[3]...

Don Salomón came from Prokurov (sometimes transliterated Proskorov or Prokorov), a town in the Russian province of Podolia, in what is now the Ukraine. He was, therefore, a *podólier* as people from that area were called. Don Salomón's family had sheep and vineyards in

---

[3] We are Rosenvasser, whereas rosewater would be Rosenwasser, with a w.

Russia. Most probably, says Abi, the land was registered in the name of someone else, a non-Jew. But another time he tells me that when the czar forbade the Jews from owning land, don Salomón did not want to become a shopkeeper and he chose to come to Argentina to work the land.

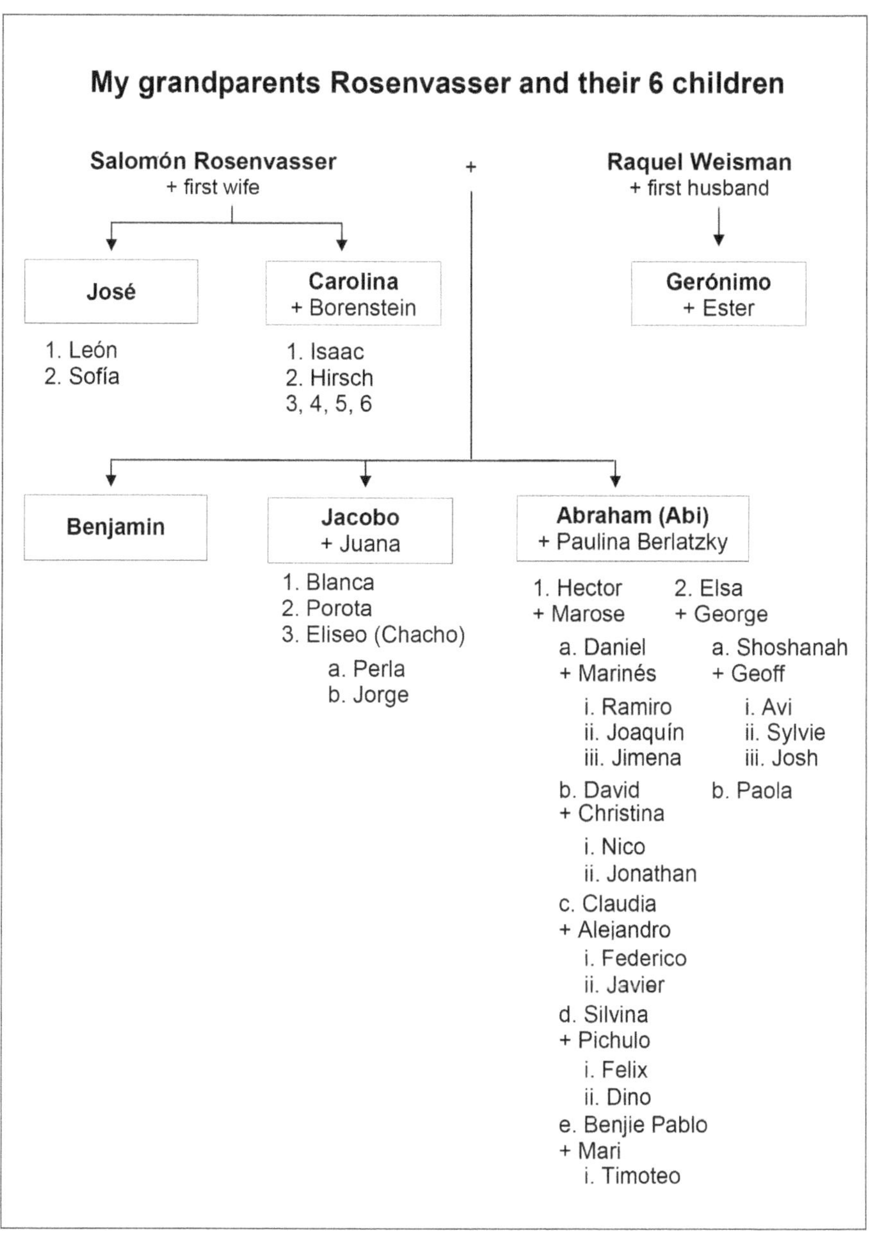

My grandparents, Raquel and Salomón Rosenvasser

Abi's mother was from Kamenetz Podolski, also a podólier. In the immigration register she appears as Rachel Weisman.[4] Despite the fact that the translation into Spanish is Raquel, in some documents she appears as Rosa. (I was born soon after she died and was given the middle name Raquel). Abi says: "Mother's father was a rabbi but he did not practice." Another time he says: "Mother's father was very well read, semi yeshiva bocher[5]; he fasted on Mondays and Thursdays, but he ate some dates, it wasn't a total fast like on Yom Kippur."[6]

Don Salomón and doña Raquel got married (they were both widowers) and they left for Argentina. He was 28 years old, with two children from his first marriage (to a certain Flora Eppel): 8-year-old

---

[4] This matter of colors in the surnames is curious: the red Roitman, the white Weisman; and in the case of my huband's parents, the father's white (Feher, in Hungarian) and the mother's black (Schwartz, in German).

[5] Term used to describe a scholar of the sacred texts.

[6] Day of Atonement.

José and 1½-year-old Carolina, or Guise as they called her (registered as Gissée). Doña Raquel was 20 years old with a 2-year-old son, Gerónimo (registered as Gessechen; probably Gershon). I don't know where this came from, that he was 28 and she was 20, because I have only Abi's word for it. But the immigration registry (of which I saw a copy in Carlos Casares[7] in 1991 during the celebration of the 100 years of the Colonia Mauricio) says something totally different! It says Salomón was 45 years old and Raquel 28 when they arrived, and that José was 18, Carolina 5 and Gerónimo 6. So the only number that coincides with Abi's version is the age difference of approximately one year between Carolina and Gerónimo.[8] In Colonia Mauricio in Argentina, three more sons were born: Benjamin in 1892, Jacobo in 1894 and Abraham in 1898. Benjamin died young. Like the majority of immigrant families, this one was a conglomeration of siblings, half-siblings and step-siblings.

Abi's father Salomón "told how in the escape from Russia they had crossed a river that marked the border (probably the Danube), by boat, at night. The border guard had fired a shot, but that was all. They went to Vienna, then Paris for two months, and from there to Le Havre, where they got on a boat of the German Lloyd company. The trip took several months, during which they ate potatoes and herring. They didn't eat meat because, although the ship carried cows in the holds, there was no *shoijet* (butcher) to kill them according to ritual laws."[9] According to Abi they arrived in Buenos Aires "a few days after the revolution, when the Unión Cívica (a political party) splintered into the Unión

---

7 Courtesy of Susana Sigwald Carioli, Director of the Instituto Histórico Antonio Maya, Carlos Casares.

8 My tendency is to believe Abi's version since, lacking a common language and script, the miscommunication between the new arrivals and the staff in the office of immigration was horrendous. In the arrival registry it says that Salomón and Raquel did <u>not</u> read or write. My interpretation, given that they owned a Talmud written in Idisch (that is now in my library), is that they did, yes, know how to read but in Idisch, which uses Hebrew letters and numbers, and not in a language with a Latin alphabet.

9 Mauricio Charchir (1976) tells of another boat, the Pampa, that brought more than 800 persons, among them a shoijet and a rabbi. But the passengers — some, at least — refused meat because the kitchen utensils were not kosher.

Cívica and the Unión Cívica Radical." But Abi was not clear on the name of the boat on which they travelled (the Rio Negro? the Rosario?) or the year in which they arrived (1890 or 1891?). The information in the immigration registry says they arrived on August 6, 1891, one year and a few days after the revolution that Abi mentions. "The revolution" is that of July 26, 1890, when the Union Cívica rises against president Juarez Celman; the Unión Cívica Radical, formed by Leandro Alem after the revolution, becomes the party of president-to-be Yrigoyen. What is of interest here is how Abi used important dates in Argentinian history and politics (the origin of yrigoyenismo in this case) as memory-markers.

In Abi's words, "When they arrived they settled into the meager rooms of what was then the Hotel de Inmigrantes and from there they went straight to Colonia Mauricio in the County of 9 de Julio. There were about 100 families that settled into groups centered around the main quarters of two ranches *(cascos de estancia)*: La Alice and El Algarrobo *(The Carob Tree)*. Alíce (pronounced with the accent on the i and with the final e voiced) was the name of the wife of the Englishman or Scotsman, Smith,[a] who had sold[10] the property to the Jewish Agency."[11] Later on, in the first years of the XXth century, the estancias La Esperanza and Santo Tomás were annexed to the Colonia in order to have enough land to distribute among the sons and sons-in-law of the colonists. By then, Colonia Mauricio spanned 44,000 hectares (about 100,000 acres).

The Rosenvasser family lived in Alice, in a place called Quince Ranchos *(Fifteen Huts)*, which in reality, said Abi, were only five.[12] Abi did his first two years of school right there in Quince Ranchos, under

---

[10] According to present-day information, the property belonged to Waldemar Laussen. Smith was the name of a nearby town and, surely, the name of the original owner of the land. There were other Britishers in the area; for example the estancia Santo Tomás, acquired a few years later for the Colonia, belonged to a family called Drysdale.

[11] This is the Jewish Colonization Agency, colloquially called La Jewish or La JCA (pronounced *eeka*). The JCA will be discussed in the next section, dealing with the agrarian colonization. Colonia Mauricio is the first of 14 colonies (it depends somewhat on how one counts them) founded by the JCA in Argentina and Brazil.

[12] It was group 67 in Alice.

the tutelage of Shimshon Yoguel, who apparently "boxed their ears if they didn't pay attention. The children used to climb the trees to eat the fruit and one day one of them choked on the pit of a peach and he cried and cried. Shimshon put him into the sulky *(horse-drawn cart)*," instructing Abi to hit him on the back. And so they went, the three of them — Shimshon driving, the boy screaming, Abi hitting him on the back — to look for help. With the jolts of the racing sulky, the pit dislodged and, finally, the boy ejected it.

After a year or two in the local school, the children began to go further afield, to the school that served the whole Alice complex. There were two teachers there: Nisensohn, and the teacher of Hebrew and

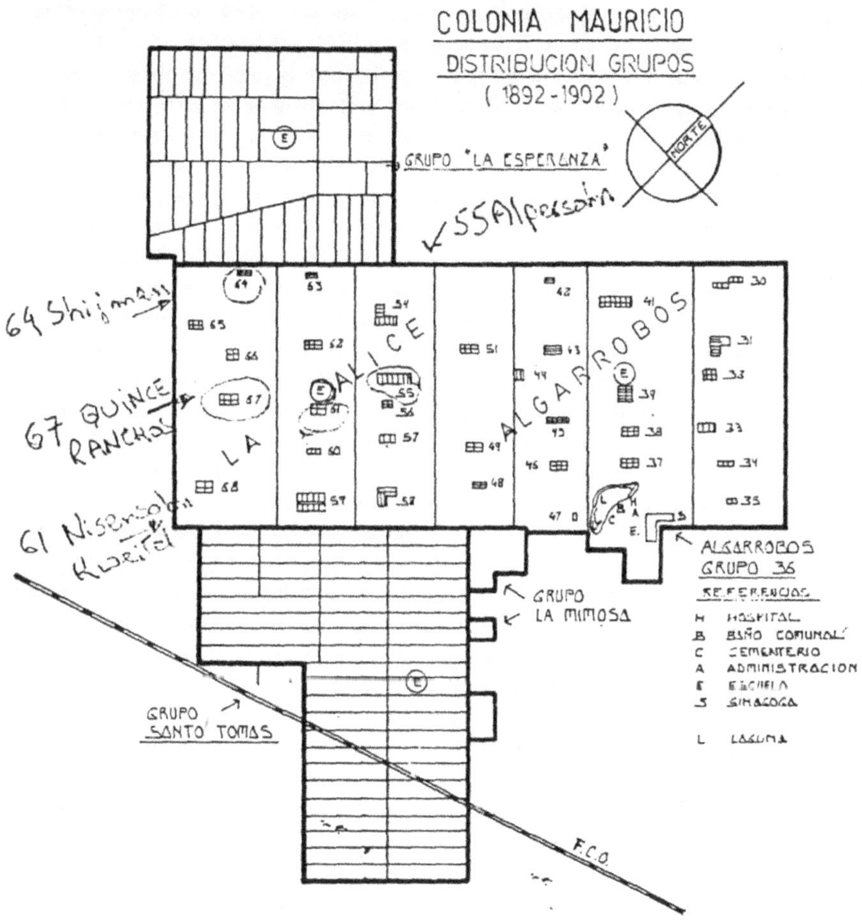

Plan of Colonia Mauricio

Talmud.[13] "Nisensohn had done his training in Buenos Aires and was a very good teacher." The first teachers in the Colonia, who taught the children Spanish and Idisch[14], were recruited by agents of the Baron Hirsch in Morocco; they spoke a somewhat nasal Spanish, with traces of French and, for sure, had no knowledge of local modes of expression. Simultaneously, La Jewish sent 15-year-olds to Buenos Aires (among them Nisensohn) to train as teachers that would have an Argentinian degree.

Abi went to the school in Alice on horseback; at first, riding bareback with his brother Jacobo, both on the same horse. Later on he had his own horse. "What was it called?" "It had no name," he responds. The school in Alice was a league-and-a-half from Quince Ranchos; that is about seven-and-a-half kilometers (a league is a measure of distance commonly used in the countryside: one league is 5 kilometers, about 50 city blocks).

The school in Alice only went as far as fourth grade. For the higher grades Abi went to Algarrobo where there were buildings suitable for a school. El Algarrobo was 5 leagues away, that is, 25 kilometers. Abi went there only about 3 months; he lived with a family, whereas Jacobo went back and forth on horseback every day. "Who motivated you to be professionals, to go and study in Buenos Aires?" I ask. "The teachers themselves," he answers.

So it was that Benjamin (who was not the youngest even though he was called Benjamin, but the oldest of the three brothers born in Argentina) and Jacobo[b] went to Buenos Aires, as did Abi, to do 6th grade in the school Bernardino Rivadavia and high school in the Nicolás Avellaneda.[15] Together with Benjamín he boarded with the family Sonnenberg. On another occasion he tells me he ate at the house

---

13 Probably Avreiml Rozenfeld, known as the "Rebe Avreiml" (Rebe means rabbi or, in this case, preceptor or teacher).

14 The word Idisch comes from Juden (or Yiden) Deutsch; it is a composite of tongues: 70% German, 25% Hebrew and 5% Slaico. Some call it "jargon".

15 According to Osías Shijman ("Colonización Judia en la Argentina," Buenos Aires, 1980, edición del autor), they were students together in the elementary school in Alice (p. 36) and also in the secondary school Nicolás Avellaneda (p. 102).

of the Sonnenbergs and lived with Benjamín in the house of a Belgian, non-Jewish family. Wherever they lived, the fact is that Benjamín died in Abi's arms, during the flu epidemic, I believe. "It is very, very painful" says Abi. "What I remember from those days is how Mother suffered. It pains me to remember. I don't want to talk about it anymore." Benjamín is the only member of the Rosenvasser family who is buried in the Jewish cemetery of Colonia Mauricio[16] — the cemetery that is on a hill, next to the Laguna *(pond)* Algarrobo.

Here lie the first dead
of Colonia Mauricio.

May their dreams of work
and human dignity
rest in peace.

Benjamin's tombstone lines 5 and 6: ... Biniamin bar Eliezer Rozinvasir ...

---

16 This is the first cemetery of the Jewish community in Argentina. It was established to bury the colonos (inhabitants of the Colonia) who died in the huge storm that hit soon after they arrived.

Don Salomón "had 200 hectares sown with barley, oats, wheat, alfalfa. There were peons[17] who helped with the work; they slept and ate in the barn. Ploughing was done with horses." According to my present readings[18] it seems the plowing was done with oxen.

The robbery, version 1: As Abi tells it, a man came on horseback. Salomón went out of the house to confront him, armed with the door-bar. Abi, who was a small child, went out through the back door with his mother, lantern in hand, to go through the high grass to warn the neighbors. The man slashed don Salomón in the face with a knife and "he fled, taking with him a horse that he stole from us. My father (don Salomón) was held in custody by the police because they thought he had killed the man and hidden his body. But then our horse came back, covered in blood, and they realized the man must have escaped."

The robbery, version 2: In another version of the robbery that I heard many years later,[c] the sly gaucho had come to steal, not a horse, but Carolina. Rosenvasser did kill him and the body was in a ditch. But the neighbors protected Salomón, and that's how the other story was invented. Abi's story must be what he was told, because he was just a child — maybe 10 years old…

When I heard this story I was shook up. But now that I'm reading the book by Marcos Alpersohn, "Colonia Mauricio" (1922), finally translated from Idisch by Eliahu Toker and published on the occasion of the hundred years of the founding of the Colonia, I find a whole chapter ("Savages invade the colony and attack women") describing kidnappings and rapes.

---

[17] Salaried workers. It was stipulated that they could only be hired for the harvest; plowing and sowing had to be done by the colonos and their family. The peons were usually gauchos, the nomads of the pampas.

[18] My present readings are mostly from two books: the one by Alpersohn, colono from Mauricio, contemporary of my grandfather don Salomón, gives a taste of the atmosphere in those first years of the colonization (Marcos Alpersohn "Colonia Mauricio," 1922 en idish. Traducción, introducción y notas de Eliahu Toker); the book by Shijman, contemporary of my father, Abi, helps us reconstruct the atmosphere of the childhood of that first generation born on Argentinian soil. (It came as a surprise to me, upon reading Shijman's book, to realize that he was the gentleman we used to go and visit in his pharmacy when I was small and we vacationed in Necochea.)

The robbery, version 3: Boris Garfunkel tells the story in his book "My Life" ("Narro mi vida," p. 292–296). The Garfunkel family lived in Quince Ranchos,[d] where their field was next to that of Rosenvasser.[19] "The intruder tried to gain access through a window. Thrusting his hand, he touched the sleeping body of Mauricio [the little son of Boris] who was spending the night with the Rosenvasser family because his mother was sick. Then Rosenvasser took courage, opened the door and went out to confront the intruder armed with a thick bar with which he hit the robber, who, in turn, took out his knife. Rosenvasser's shouts for help woke his wife, who stole out of the house and called their neighbor Leiser Guirstel (Lázaro Gerstel), who shot his gun several times and so caused the assailant to flee. Rosenvasser lay unconscious due to a knife wound that went from above his eyebrow to the front of his bald head. After getting first aid, he was taken to Carlos Casares."

Don Boris (Garfunkel), says Abi, once bit the hand of don Salomón in tremendous anger. The incident was due to some horses of Rosenvasser that got into the cornfield of Garfunkel to eat his fresh corn.[20] Or was it the other way around and the incident occurred because Rosenvasser had confiscated in his corral some horses that belonged to Garfunkel that were stomping his (Rosenvasser's) planted area? Whatever caused the incident, the truth, says Abi, is that "the old man bit the hand of my father [Salomón Rosenvasser] and left him with a scar forever. Later, Garfunkel was treated by doctor Weksler and it seems he was cured of his bad temper"(¡!).

This tale finds its complement in the description of the personalities of Garfunkel and Rosenvasser given by Alpersohn (1922): "Boruj Garfinkel [sic]," says Alpersohn, "… idealist and a free spirit, … left behind [in Russia] riches and a huge and illustrious family … Boruj was the head of the Quince Ranchos, sort of like its president; … he steered the communal ship like a true captain." Another of the leaders, writes

---

[19] This can be seen in the map of the plots of land that is in the Jewish Museum of the synagogue on Libertad street in Buenos Aires.

[20] It seems this type of incident was relatively common: phenomenal disputes because one person's animals trod on the planted fields of another …

Alpersohn, "was the peaceful Shloime Rozenvaser [sic], a deep, erudite, Jew with large eyes, open, clear, candid. His principal task was to calm the other two [one of them being Garfunkel] when they spat burning lava talking about the oppression of the colonos by the directors … He would contain them, calm them and prevent them from taking impulsive steps that could lead them all astray."

Alpersohn tells about the cultural differences within the colony that caused him to move from Algarrobos to Alice. The colonos from Algarrobos, he says, were mostly orthodox, observers of the law and very hard working. But Alice was the thinking and rebellious center of the Colonia. The leaders, among them Garfunkel and Rosenvasser, were from Quince Ranchos, which is why Quince Ranchos was considered the "capital" of Alice and was nicknamed "Moscow." What "Moscow" decided, the rest of Alice respected. In Alpersohn's view "It was the most beautiful and vital goup within the Colonia." He describes a scene on the eve of Pesaj (Passover) in 1894, when the colonos get together to bake matzot[21] in Quince Ranchos, where there is an oven. "Tall and scholarly … Leizer Nisensohn[22] was in charge of the flour; red-headed and bare-footed … Berl Rabinovich[23] was in charge of the water; Roizenwaser [sic] and Alpersohn kneaded the dough."

Matters of health and hygiene were always problematic. "The physician of the Colonia, a good doctor who diagnosed Jacobo's tifus, didn't have a degree because when he was a student in Russia he was sent to Siberia. From there he fled and came to Argentina. After some time the JCA wanted their physicians to have degrees and the good doctor had to abandon his post." Here I find inconsistencies, because it seems the tifus epidemic was in 1892 and ever since the birth of Jacobo in 1894 there was a degreed physician in the Colonia.

Perhaps Abi conflated Jacobo's illness with hearsay about doctor Joffe, who was the first, much-loved, non-degreed permanent physician

---

21 Unleavened bread that symbolizes the haste with which the Jews left Egypt, led by Moses: There was not enough time to let leavened bread rise.

22 The father of the teacher.

23 The grandfather of the musician from Les Lutiers (an excellent humorous musical group).

of the colony. Before Joffe, in the early days of the Colonia, a certain doctor Rhodes came every so often from Pehuajó (a town in the neighboring county, now famous for being the birthplace of Manuelita — the beloved turtle in a children's song). Eventually the Baron sent a physician from Europe, Teófilo Weksler, who arrived in Colonia Mauricio in March 1894. In due course, Weksler got tired of the machinations of the administration and left. This meant the colonos had two options: treat their malady at home, or go to the hospital in far-off Buenos Aires. This was really unsatisfactory because there were many accidents: the harvesting and threshing machinery was ancient and the colonos were totally unskilled in its use.

But they learnt, they learnt. My brother tells me that during a trip we took to the South of Argentina in 1940, in tandem with friends,[e] one of the cars developed problems and Abi got underneath the chassis and fixed it. Abi was not precisely what one would call 'technologically astute,' so at the time, my brother marveled aloud about Abi's success. Abi's comment: "The mechanism is the same as in a harvesting machine."

The confrontations with the administrators were constant and frustrating for the colonos. They felt mocked, humiliated and robbed. The directors in the Buenos Aires office and the administrators of the Colonia changed often: First, there was a German officer and an English colonel; after that, two Russian Jews; then a pair of Frenchmen; then a Lithuanian. All this in just 5 years. One of the main grievances was that the JCA would not give the colonos the deeds to their plots of land. Abi says: "Raitzin was the leader[24] of the colonos that sued the JCA to get the deeds. The colonos won. The JCA did not want to give them the deeds so they would not sell the land." Actually, from the standpoint of the JCA this made some sense; but from the standpoint of the colonos it was tantamount to serfdom.

Aside from Jacobo, the other member of the family I remember well is Gerónimo. The only time I saw Abi cry was when Gerónimo died. "Gerónimo had some land parcels; he lost everything during the

---

[24] Actually, Alpersohn went with Raitzin to see the general directors in Buenos Aires.

depression of '29. In Buenos Aires he was a *cuentenik* (door-to-door salesman). He sold silk stockings and earned his living with difficulty." Gerónimo married Ester Yoguel, my Tia Ester, who had matzos baked especially for us for Pesaj and made us sweet fruit wine and white cheese beigelej. How I loved that white wine! When Abi complained that it had too much alcohol, Ester said "No, Abraham, no; it's only fruit; I don't put in any alcohol."

The Yoguel family included Shimshon (Sansón), Abi's teacher in Quince Ranchos.[f] Ester and Gerónimo didn't have any children. When he died, Jacobo and Abi took over caring for Ester's expenses. In those days we went to visit her every so often. She continued to make Jewish food for us but every year it came out worse. It was my first encounter with culinary deterioration in old age, a phenomenon I'm starting to experience myself…

When Salomón died, his eldest son, José,[g] who had always been very jealous of his half-brother Gerónimo, didn't want him to be part of the division of the inheritance. So it was divided into four: José, Carolina, Jacobo, Abi. After that, Jacobo and Abi divided their part in three with Gerónimo (who had the same mother but was not a blood son of Salomón).

Guise (Carolina), the aborted-kidnap sister, "fell in love with the gringo [the Russian] Borenstein who played the guitar and sang nicely." (Clearly, Abi didn't have much respect or admiration for this gringo.) They married and had six children,[h] among them Hirsch, so named to honor the Barón, a common practice in the colonias.

Don Salomón asked the JCA for two more plots of land, one for his son-in-law Borenstein and another for his stepson Gerónimo. In the lottery only Borenstein got a lot; but he didn't want to share it with Gerónimo. Years later he (together with José) was against giving Gerónimo a portion of the inheritance of don Salomón. I suppose he acted in the name of Carolina, who was the heir. Abi told this story repetitively; it weighed on him.

Many years later, Abi's years in the Colonia reverberated through Manuel (Manucho) Mujica Láinez. In his speech in 1980 on the occasion of Abi's election to the Argentine Academy of Letters, Mujica talks about:

"… the country boy born in the fifteen huts … who tells of going on horseback — mounting bareback in the frosty mornings, trying not to touch the barbed wires with his knees that were naked under the poncho, — to a school of the Jewish Colonization Agency,

A young Abi

where in the mornings the teaching was in Hebrew and in the afternoon, in Spanish. He had, however, the advantage of having a father who, although a colono, a farmer, knew the atavic language which he used, as if singing psalms, for reading to him — in the intimacy of the modest house surrounded by the immense isolation of the pampa — the venerable texts that narrate the hopes, glories, the lyricism, disappointments and tragedies of his ancient race. There, then, in that cluster of huts, among gauchos, cattle and winding tilled land, but also among people who kept their famous legends and stories as if they protected from the wind some marvelous ancient lamps, the vocation of scholar and artist was born in Abraham Rosenvasser.

The young boy, flexible, made of angles and penetrating eyes, at the same time ironical and thoughtful, came to Buenos Aires, like so many others, following the starry map of provincial dreams. His ambitions were rooted in his thirst for knowledge … for he had learnt how to control and ride the courses at the University with the same skill with which he rode his horse, galloping in the pampas."

Manucho and Abi had met in 1979, when Mujica Láinez was writing his novel "El escarabajo" *(The Beetle)* and he contacted Abi to consult him on some egyptological matters in the book.

2. History of the Jewish colonies of the Barón Hirsch

The history of the Jewish colonies of the Barón Hirsch is very well-known to some but totally unknown to others. I recount it here for the many who do not know it, for it is a truly compelling story.

I'll start with the Barón Hircsh, one of the three Barons of the XIXth century who used their vast fortunes to better the living conditions of the Jews of Europe. The other two barons, Edmund de Rothschild and Horace de Günzburg, appear briefly later on in this story.[25]

---

[25] Although they well deserve to have their individual stories told. See, for example, "The Four Winds of Heaven," written by the granddaughter of a Günzburg, Monique Raphel High (1980); and "The Rothschilds" by Frederic Morton (1961).

The Baron Moritz von Hirsch, a Bavarian German, was born in
1813. He descended from a rich family of "court bankers."[26] He went to
work in an international banking firm where his business sense enabled
him to advance rapidly. He married Clara Bischoffsheim, daughter
of one of the owners of the firm, and was named director of the Paris
branch, which is the reason why we know him by the French version of
his name, Maurice de Hirsch. Clara and Mauricio had only one child,
a son, Lucien, who died at age 31. These names — Mauricio, Clara and
Lucien — were perpetuated as names of colonies in Argentina.

The middle of the XIXth century heralds the age of railways throughout the world. In Europe, Hirsch concludes the construction of the line
that links Europe with the Balkans (the famous Orient Express). This
work and his trips make him aware of the miserable living conditions of
the Jews of Eastern Europe and Russia. He attempts to intervene with
the Czar to provide schools for the education of the Russian Jews and
so enable them to better their lot. But he fails. He then forges another
plan: to help the Jews leave Russia, buy land for them to settle in, and
turn them into farmers. In his scheme it was essential that the Jews be
willing to do manual and physical work.

In order to manage such a project and the enormous amounts of
money he invests in it, Hirsch founds the Jewish Colonization Agency
(JCA) in London in 1891.[27]

---

[26] Court bankers were those Jews who handled the financial matters of princes and
kings, giving them credit to keep their armies and feed their love of luxury. These
court bankers, through their ties with far-flung Jewish communities via family and
friends, could provide the money needed by royalty when they traveled outside their
own territories. In return for these services, court bankers were exempt from many
of the restrictions imposed upon their coreligionaries: They could, for example, live
outside the ghettoes and carry arms. Court bankers existed primarily in Germany; see
the history of these Jews in Germany excellently portrayed in the book by Amos Elon
"The Pity of It All" (2002).

[27] Barón Hirsch died in 1896, five years after founding the JCA, but his wife Clara,
actively continued with her husband's projects. La JCA still exists today, dedicated
foremost to projects within Israel. In prior years JCA's projects outside Argentina and
Brazil included agricultural colonies in the United States, Canada, Cyprus, Turkey and
Palestine as well as vocational education and financial credits and loans for the Jews of
Eastern Europe.

Emigration as the solution to the problem of the Jews in Russia had been discussed in St. Petersburg, in a meeting of the leadership of the Jewish population.[28] Opinions were divided, but the majority was not in favor of officially supporting a massive emigraton effort. The Russian government had no objections to Jews leaving the country, and did not put any obstacles in their way; in fact, it is said the advisor to the czar proposed a solution by thirds: "Let one third of the Jewish population emigrate, one third assimilate and we eliminate the remaining third." Therefore, in the beginning, emigration was a matter of individual initiative for each family. Going to Palestine, which was the wish of many, was not feasible because of the restrictions imposed by the Turks. The other destination was the United States of America, where many Russian Jews had family members already established. Between 1881 and 1888 the emigration to the United States numbers 150,000 Russian Jews.

In this framework, a group of 120 families who had heard about the open-door attitude of Argentina towards immigration had bought land in the province of Santa Fe via a certain Hernandez in Paris. The story of their arrival in Argentina in 1890 on board the ship Weser[29] is very sad and full of suffering. Robbed, unprotected, not knowing the language, in the middle of the countryside they wait for weeks for the expected transportation to the promised lands. Thirty children, or more, die of hunger. Having heard about this situation, doctor Guillermo Loewenthal meets them in the train station where they are stranded (Palacios in the province of Santa Fe), and immediately sets to work to find help.

Doctor Loewenthal is an important character in this colonization movement. He had arrived in Argentina to inspect the colonies that existed in the country (all non-Jewish at that time), a task with which he was charged by the Argentinian government through its embassy in Paris. Loewenthal was a physician, well-known in Europe, who

---

[28] The most prestigious leader in St. Petersburg was Baron Edmond de Günzburg. Together with Hirsch and Rothschild, Günzburg integrates the threesome of monyed, philantropic barons who attended to the wellbeing of the Jews in czarist Russia.

[29] The story of the colonos who arrived in 1890 in the ship Weser is told by Lázaro Schallman ("Los pioneros de la colonizacion judia en la Argentina, 1969).

was actively interested in matters of education and hygiene. He had important contacts; in particular, with Barón Maurice de Hirsch, the great philanthropist, whom he approaches to ask for economic assistance for the immigrants of the Weser. The aid is granted and Loewenthal uses it to establish the immigrants in Santa Fe, in what will become known as Colonia Moisesville.[30]

Although Moisesville is the first Jewish colony in Argentina[31], and it was founded with financial help from the Barón, it pre-dates the Barón's colonization project. Nevertheless it does constitute the vanguard of Jewish agricultural colonization in Argentina.

Driven by Loewenthal's and other independent reports, the Barón decides to go ahead with his project in Argentina. He charges Loewenthal with the acquisition of land. The JCA acquires legal status in Argentina in 1892. So begins the ambitious project of re-establishment (in Argentina) and what today we would call re-training (for agricultural work) of Russian Jews. The plan was to begin by establishing 25,000 Jews in the Argentinian countryside and increasing the number every year, to a total of 3 millon in 25 years of colonization.[32] In point of fact, Jewish immigration in Argentina in the years prior to the first world war (which are the heyday of the JCA) never exceeded 15,000 a year (actually, with ups and downs, the average was about 5,000 per year) of

---

30 So called for the biblical Moses, who liberated the Jews from their servitude in Egypt and led them to the promised land in Palestine. It could also be that it was named Moisesville in honor of Barón Hirsch (since his name is Moritz = Mauricio = Mosché = Moisés).

31 Before the arrival of the Weser there were Jewish immigrants in the cities. Their number was small. But they became sadly famous because of the white slave trade, an infamous chapter in the early Jewish settlement in Argentina, that dovetails the history of the Weser. A Polish mafia had set up a system importing Jewish Polish women, bringing them to Argentina under the false pretense that they were coming to get married to single settlers and start an honest family. Some of the women of the Weser, says Avni (1969, p.123), to avoid hunger and uncertainty, ended up in those whorehouses in Buenos Aires. These white slave trade societies, the most famous of which was called Migdal (i.e. the Star), last into the 1930s; their infamous story has been told by Gerardo Bra (1982).

32 These numbers come from Simon Dubnow, "History of the Jews in Russia and Poland," Philadelphia 1918, Vol II p.419 cited by Morton Winsberg, in his monograph (1963).

which an estimated ten percent went to the colonies. In 1913, on the eve of the first world war, the population of the colonies was 26,000.[33]

In the meantime, the situation of the prospective immigrants in Russia and Rumania worsens rapidly with pogroms and laws that impose more and more restrictions. In consequence, those who manage to leave are impatient to do so immediately, and in the months of July and August 1891 six ships[34] with immigrants arrive in Argentina. The passengers are the first settlers of the first colony established by the JCA: Colonia Mauricio. Because the colonos arrived prematurely, before a proper infrastructure could be set up to receive them, Mauricio is the colony of the project whose settlers suffered the most.

The ships continue to arrive one after another: Don Pedro, Petrópolis, Itaparica, Porto Alegre, Bahía, Desterro, Paraguazú, Ceará, El Pampa. In the six months between July and December 1891, the Jewish immigrants who arrive in Argentina, destined by the JCA for the Barón Hirsch colonies, number 2,500.[35] The boats come from Germany (Bremen, Hamburg) or France (Le Havre, Bordeaux).

El Pampa came from Bordeaux, bringing more than 800 Russian Jews; their story is well-known because, as different from other journeys, this one has been well documented.[36] The Jewish immigrants from the Pampa had congregated in Constantinople. Like so many of the others who could escape from Russia, they intended to sail across the Mediterranean to go to Palestine. This they did. But the Turks had a vast empire that included Palestine and although some time earlier some Russian Jews had gained entry,[37] in 1891 the Ottoman empire closed Jewish immigration to Palestine and the boat was sent back to

---

[33] Data inferred from the information given by H. Avni (1983) and T. Norman (1985).

[34] Among them the Tiyuca, the Lisboa (or Lissabon), the Rosario, and the Rio Negro.

[35] See Susana Sigwald Carioli (1991).

[36] See Lázaro Shallman (1972).

[37] In 1881 Eliezer Perlman, known as Ben Yehuda, emigrated to Palestine. He was a linguist, and is considered to be the father of modern Hebrew. Ben Yehuda maintained that Hebrew was the Jewish language and that the Idisch jargon had to be abandoned. As exemplar, he raised his son speaking only Hebrew, probably the first person in modern times to grow up speaking only Hebrew.

Constantinople. (Echoes of boats with Holocaust survivors that the British Empire does not allow to disembark in Palestine...).

Back in Constantinople, dismayed, they asked Barón Hirsch to allow them to go to Argentina with his groups. This is how they end up going to Marseilles on the Fressina,[38] a boat flying a French flag. From there by train to Bordeaux. And in Bordeaux they board the Pampa.

The bare-bones facts seem simple. But much went on behind the scenes. For example, the European commission in charge of selecting the emigrants puts out an order that the long black caftans must be shortened, as well as hair and beards. Some among the orthodox refuse to cut their *paies* (in Idisch; *peot* in Hebrew; these are the sideburns, long and curled)[39] and prefer to forgo the trip.

The pampistas, who were also known as *stámbuler* because of their provenance, colonized Entre Ríos[i]: Basavilbaso, Dominguez, Clara, Lucienville... The family of Abi's wife, my mother, belonged to this group; that is, my great-grandfather arrived in Istanbul from that zone in between Russia and Rumania called Besarabia.[j]

The Barón Hirsch project founded eight colonies in Argentina and two in the South of Brazil[k] between 1891 and 1913 (Moisesville, founded in 1980, is not considered part of the JCA project); after the first world war only two more were founded.[40] Although the bulk of the work buying land and settling the immigrants ended with the first

---

38 This is according to Lázaro Schallman (1972). As in almost everything that concerns that time, there exist various versions. The French boat was called Galatz, according to one of the passengers, Mauricio Charchir (1976).

39 Hair plays an important role in Judaism: the male believers do not cut (or trim) the hair that grows on their face, whereas women cut all of their hair when they get married and wear a wig or kerchief to cover their head. These practices originate, respectively, in the laws of Leviticus and in a custom from the XVth century based on the argument that hair is an erotic element that can distract men's attention and conspire against conjugal faithfulness. Remembering the story of Sampson, whose incredible strength resided in his long hair, the two traditional customs seem to symbolize the disparity between male and female power.

40 In chronological order of their founding, the colonies are: 1. Mauricio (Carlos Casares) 1891; 2. Clara (Domínguez) 1892; 3. Lucienville (Basavilbaso) 1894; 4. Philippson 1903; 5. Barón Hirsch (Rivera) 1905; 6. Santa Isabel 1908; 7. Narcisse Leven 1909; 8. Quatro Irmaos 1910; 9. Dora 1912; 10. Montefiore 1912; 11. Cohen-Oungre 1925; 12. Avigdor 1935.

world war, the JCA continued giving loans and, in general, helping the colonos. The work of the JCA in Argentina came to an end only in 1975.

Jewish colonies in Argentina and Brazil

3. The situation in Russia

What was it that caused the Russian Jews to launch themselves into the unknown in such haste? Before answering this question there is a prior one to consider: Who were these Russian Jews, where did they come from? Since the end of the XVth century there had been no Jews in Russia, for they had been banished — much as they were expulsed from Spain at about the same time. But at the end of the XVIIIth century, the reigning czarina, Catherine II, finds that the new territories she has just acquired as a consequence of the dismemberment of Poland are populated by undesirables: almost one million Jews are now residing in Russian territory. Thus is born the Pale of Settlement, proclaimed in 1772: a boundary that limits the residence of Jews to the area they inhabited prior to the partition of Poland. Henceforth, Russian Jews must live within the Pale.

During the following hundred years there are important events within the Jewish community. The coronation of czar Alexander II in 1856 heralds a period of liberating reforms that culminate in 1865 with the opening of all of Russia to Jewish craftsmen and their families. Many of these artisans establish themselves in Kiev and Moscow. At this time, also, there is a strengthening of the movement called The Enlightenment (Haskalah),[41] which advocates secular education for children, elimination of Idisch in favor of the local tongue, and learning Hebrew. Those years, also, signal the beginnings of what will be the Russian revolution, and many Jews are part of that first so-called "nihilistic" movement.

However, although lifting the restrictions gave rise to some very rich individuals and the formation of an *intelligentsia*, the vast majority of Jews continued to live in atrocious poverty, crowding, hunger and bad health. The murder of Alexander II and the access to power of his son Alexander III bring back the terror: The persecution of Jews resumes, and in 1881 and 1882 the first wave of pogroms — organized killings — occurs in the South of Russia. The very year 1882, a ukase of the czar banishes from Moscow the 20,000 Jews who live there. The exiles have to settle in the already saturated towns within the Pale. In May 1883 new laws are proclaimed that prohibit the towns within the Pale to take in more Jews than are already living there and, also, forbid Jews from owning or administering land. The freedoms obtained under the prior czar continue to be abrogated, and when Alexander III dies in 1894, his son and successor Nicholas II does not bring any respite.

---

41 This movement starts in Germany circa 1750 with Moses Mendelssohn (grandfather of the musician Felix Mendelssohn-Bartholdy). It arises in Russia in the 1820s but does not prosper at that time due to the existing oppressive czarist regimes of Alexander I and Nicholas I.

By then the family of Abi had already departed the Pale for Argentina. Kamenetz Podolski, where don Salomón came from, had been part of Poland up until the annexations of 1700, and had suffered in the sadly famous pogrom of 1600 organized by the cossack Khmelnitsky. Kherson, where doña Raquel came from, was founded in the Ukraine only in 1778, and around 1837–1841 it was colonized by Jews who worked the land, in one of three intents of the Russian government to organize Jewish colonies.[42]

During the reign of Nicholas II, the last Romanov, one pogrom follows another. They are veritable massacres, that get bloodier as the government becomes more unstable with military defeats[43] and as the clamor of the revolutionary movement gets louder. When the socialist revolution is unleashed in 1917, the czar is forced to resign in favor of

Pogroms In the Pale of Settlement 1881–1906

---

42 The other two were in the Odessa region (in 1810, in territories yielded by Turkey); and in Siberia (in 1835–37).

43 in the Russian–Japanese war.

the provisional government which, on the eve of Pesaj in March 1917, rescinds all restrictions and gives total civil liberty to the Jews.

4. The situation in Argentina

While all this was going on in Europe, Argentina was a country beginning to take shape. In Europe, the tired monarchies and empires were incubating revolutions. But America was starting from scratch, designing new countries.

In Argentina it became clear from the start that in order to have an independent country it was necessary to bring in people to work its huge, sparsely populated expanses. In the words of Sarmiento, the country was a desert that demanded settlers. Exiled in Chile during the rule of Juan Manuel de Rosas, Sarmiento writes his book "Civilización y barbarie" (*Civilization and barbarism*, 1845), where the desert stands for barbarism and European culture for civilization. This idea is echoed in the dictum of Alberdi "Gobernar es poblar" *(To govern is to settle)* formulated in his book "Bases"[44] that was so very influential in the framing of the National Constitution.

That immigration was needed to populate and develop the country was clear, but the obstacle was the matter of non-catholic immigrants, the freedom — or not — of worship. After a lengthy debate, the Asamblea Nacional Constituyente (the body that framed the constitution of the nation) approved the article that maintains the freedom of worship and signed the National Constitution into effect in 1853, in Santa Fe.

It was still necessary to provide legislation for the article on immigration. Bartolomé Mitre, the first president, was in favor of spontaneous immigration, welcoming immigrants but without governmental responsibilities. Sarmiento, the second president, was in favor of immigration promoted by the government to attract qualified immigrants (as he himself did when he "imported" teachers from the United States of America). Only in 1876, during the mandate of Nicolás Avellaneda, third president of the Republic, was it possible to pass the Law of Immigration and Colonization, that lasted for 70 years, until 1946.

---

44 "Las bases de la organización, desarrollo y progreso del pais" *(The bases of the organization, development and progress of our country)* written by J.B. Alberdi in 1852.

Two years later, in 1878–79, the "conquest of the desert" takes place. Led by Julio Roca, the conquest was a massacre of natives that ended the *malones*[45] and resulted in a considerable gain in territory for the Republic. In the language of the time, the campaigns of Roca pushed out the borders of the country, conquering the desert. From the modern perspective, the so-called desert was the land of the mapuche and the campaigns of Roca were little less than genocide, as is proclaimed today by the blood-red graffiti on the statue of Roca in Diagonal Sur in Buenos Aires. Julio Roca, having achieved fame and glory with his conquest, was elected fourth president of the Republic, after Avellaneda.

With the growth of territory thanks to the conquest of the desert, the need for immigrants had become even greater. This is precisely the time of the bloody pogroms in Russia that reverberate all over Europe. The agent of the Department of Immigration of Argentina in Paris[46] attempts to steer part of the exodus of Russian Jews towards Argentina. To this end he contacts president Roca who nominates a certain José María Bustos "honorary agent in Europe with the special charge of directing towards the Argentine Republic the Israelite emigration that has just begun in the Russian Empire." A very interesting document, indeed. Bustos' instructions are to contact the Argentinian ambassador in Paris and the leaders of the Jewish community in France, including the Great Rabbi of Paris, Zadok Kahn.

Meantime, in Russia, the Baron Horace de Günzburg, leader of the Jewish community of St. Petersburg, opposed the emigration of the Jews but fostered the founding of schools to improve life conditions of the Russian Jews via education. This was also the position taken by Barón Hirsch at the time.

---

[45] The *malones* (an Araucano word) were surprise attacks on settlements by groups of natives who killed, kidnapped, robbed and burned. The "Martín Fierro" (by José Hernández, 1872) and "La cautiva" (*The captive,* by Esteban Echeverría, 1837) tell about those violent episodes.

[46] The immigration law of 1876 created two executive arms: the Department of Immigration and the Office of Land and Colonies. The Department was charged with opening agencies in the European countries in order to publicize and organize the immigration.

5. Paris

The linking between the events in Russia and Argentina occurs in Paris. The Argentinian Office of Immigration had its central European bureau in Paris. The Alliance Israelite Universelle, the world's most important organization of the Jewish community, was located in Paris. Also in Paris lived the two barons who, together with Günzburg, played a preponderant role in the Jewish emigration from Russia.

In 1887, faced with total expulsion from Russia, representatives of affected Jewish communities got together to consider three alternatives for emigration: Palestine, the United States and Africa.[47] It was rumored that Baron Edmond de Rothschild, in charge of the French branch of the Rothschild banks, was interested in helping with the immigration into Palestine. So an emissary was dispatched to Paris to meet with Rothschild. The mission was not successful, but in Paris the emissary hears about the explicit invitation to the Jewish immigrants from the president of Argentina, Julio Roca. Contact with the agency of the Departament of Immigration and Colonization of Argentina reveals that immigrants can buy land to settle there. Which they do. This is the ill-fated acquisition of land that caused so many problems to the Jews who arrived in Argentina on the Weser.

The Alliance Israélite Universelle was founded in Paris in 1860 to protect the human rights of Jews in the country in which they lived. It was a unique entity with worldwide reach. Barón Hirsch regarded the educational activity of the Alliance as being enormously important and he contributed substantially to its support. What is more, Hirsch had the idea of using the model of the Alliance Universelle to better the conditions of Jewish life in Russia and offered the czar funding to implement a plan that included the creation of schools. But the czar refuses the offer unless the funds can be administered by his government. This is unacceptable to Hirsch. He finally recognizes that the only possibility

---

47 England suggested Uganda, one of its protectorates in East Africa, a country rich in natural resources, with ample space and no tradition of antisemitism. Sixteen years later, during the sixth Zionist congress in 1903, this possibility was considered once again and Theodor Hertzl supported it. He emphasized, however, that it would be a provisional solution. See Greenberg (1976) Vol II p.183.

for the Russian Jews to live their lives with dignity is to emigrate from Russia. This, too, is the conclusion reached by the other baron, Günzburg, who ends up being on the selection committee that chooses, in St. Petersburg, the acceptable candidates for settling the future Barón Hirsch colonies in Argentina.

Why didn't Hirsch finance the immigration to Palestine? It's not as if he hadn't considered doing so. In 1891, in a meeting held in Paris with Rothschild, Hirsch explains that he is not opposed to colonizing Palestine. It's just that he considers Argentina to be more suitable and prefers to concentrate his efforts there. So Rothschild supported the Zionist scheme and the two philanthropists were henceforth careful not to tread on each others' toes and kept their projects separate. Perhaps Hertzl would have been able to convince Hirsch to support immigration to Palestine. But the timing wasn't right: Hertzl, with his vision of the Promised Land but no concrete plans, goes to see Hirsch in 1895, when Hirsch is already totally committed to the agricultural colonies in Argentina. Moreover, Hirsch dies a few months after they meet…

6. Coda

What is the balance of the Jewish agricultural colonization in Argentina? Was the Barón Hirsch entreprise a success or a failure? From one standpoint it was a failure: the large number of immigrants proposed by Barón Hirsch never materialized and nothing remains of the huge effort to found a Jewish home based on agriculture. As in Abi's family, the first generation born in Argentina left for the urban centers, eventually taking along parents and siblings and leaving the land in the hands of non-Jews.

But from a human standpoint it was a tremendous success: that first generation settled in an Argentina full of possibilities, and peppered it with teachers, writers, musicians[48], businessmen and professionals.

Within Argentinian agriculture there are two interesting contributions from the Jewish colonies. The first is the introduction of cooperativism, reminiscent of the *moshavim* that would be created later on in

---

[48] Daniel Barenboim, pianist and orchestra conductor of international renown, is grandson of colonos from Mauricio.

Israel. The second is the introduction of sunflowers into crop farming. This is a somewhat humorous story. The sunflower was initially introduced in Argentina into the Colonia Mauricio because the colonos missed chewing the seeds. In the Ukraine, it was usual to carry a handful in the pocket and, every so often, extract a seed, bite it to separate the shell that was thrown away and eat the inside pip. Somewhat, I suppose, like a smoker lights a cigarette. To feed this "vice" they planted sunflowers. And most certainly also to surround themselves with yellow fields like those of the old homeland, which was the region in Russia where sunflowers were grown. Some time ago we saw a film, "Everything is Illuminated," in which an American kid goes to Odessa to see the land of his grandparents. There are some wondrous scenes of vast fields planted with sunflowers and a house totally surrounded by those huge yellow flowers. It's this flower from the Ukrainian fields that the *podólier* imported to Argentina. For nostalgic reasons. Yet in time they commercialized the production with such success that it became an important staple for the country.

I think it's funny that Abi, who liked to eat nuts and raisins, always had dried fruit in the pockets of his grey flannel suit.[49] Every now and then he'd stick his hand into the pocket of his jacket and extract a couple of nuts or raisins that he ate — just as if he were a Ukrainian eating sunflower seeds.

Notes a–k

[a] Within this area of British landowners (at train station Corbett) was the estancia of the grandfather of my best friend from my English school, Mildred Corbett Dawney. In that estancia, Santa Elena, Mildred and I were intensely happy, galloping on our horses without limits of time, space or speed!

[b] Abi says: "From Buenos Aires, Jacobo did not send money to our mother: everything he earned went to his fiancée Juana Ellman. Jacobo lived at the Ellmans' where everything they bought — vegetables, fruit — was rotten." Juana Ellman had been the girlfriend of Benjamin. She then was Jacobo's

---

[49] Bought at James Smart on Calle Florida. Or in the really old times, at McHardy Brown.

girlfriend and they married: Jacobo was very young. Juana, older than he, "ruined his life; always jealous." I remember when my cousin Chacho (Eliseo), the son of Jacobo and Juana, got married. After his parents separated, Chacho always lived with Jacobo. The two of them, Chacho and Jacobo, asked my mother to act as mother-of-the-groom, going into the synagogue with Chacho and the whole nine yards; for them, Juana did not exist. My mother accepted, and the letters with curses that arrived from Juana were terrifying.

[c] This I heard from the wife of Leonardo Tarán (whose maiden name is Lida, a family from Quince Ranchos).

[d] The family Kweitel was also from the Colonia, from the "group of the heretics" in Alice. Nelly Kweitel tells me (in 2001) that when they were children they always spent their holidays in their grandparents' property in Colonia Mauricio. It still belongs to the family and they go every so often.

The granddaughter of don Boris, Norita Garfunkel, was my schoolmate in kindergarten and the lower grades in the English school in Belgrano, St. Margaret's. When she was a young woman (perhaps 18?) her grandfather and parents offered in her honor a grand formal ball that I attended (together with Edith Schellemberg), long dress and all. I imagine don Boris was re-creating the environment of his childhood in the house of his moneyed family in Russia.

[e] The family Maquiavelo.

[f] In 1992 a very pleasant young writer came to see me in the museum in San Diego (the Reuben Fleet Science Center), concerning one of our exhibitions that he wanted to take to Buenos Aires (something that <u>almost</u> came about). He brought greetings from his mother, whose mother had been a Yoguel from the Colonia, sister of Tía Ester. I lost sight of him …

[g] José had, among other children, a son León, physician in the Navy, and a daughter Sofía. Abi told me that someone from this family (I lost the reference) converted to Catholicism and, when his mother died, he put in the newspaper a notice full of crosses even though the mother had never left Judaism.

[h] They had 2 girls and 4 boys, among them Isaac, who worked with Jacobo in the Rosenvasser Obstetric Clinic on Avenida San Martín (where a vast portion of the Jewish children of my generation were born). Also Hirsch, who

has 3 sons who are professionals; today, at age 90, he goes to his social club several times a week with his current woman friend, to dance folkloric dances.

[i] In January 1981 I went with Clarita Mallar (Pechersky) on a visit to the colonies of Entre Ríos. We left her country home "Los tilos" *(The Linden Trees)* in Colón, Entre Rios, with Clarita driving her car. What follows is taken from my notes during that trip.

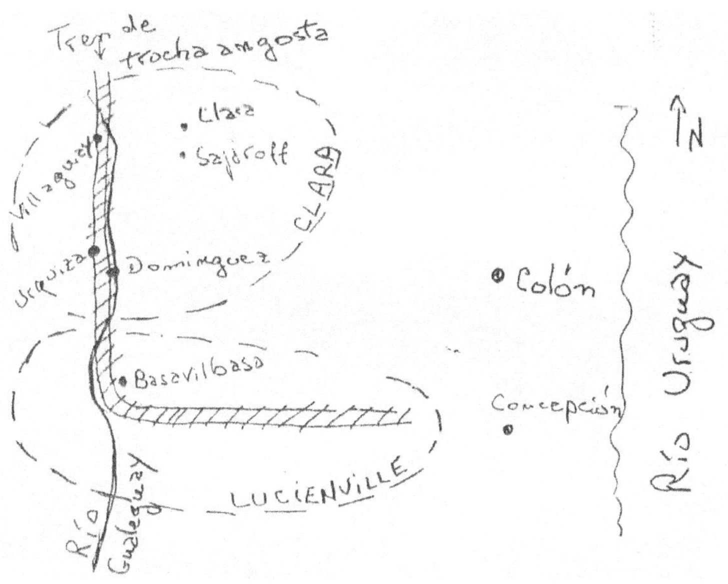

Our route of my January 1981 visit to the colonies of Entre Ríos with childhood friend Clarita Mallar (Pechersky)

We headed for Villaguay passing by thistles one meter high, tamarinds with whitewashed trunks, *ceibos* (coral trees) in bloom, olive trees, weeping willows, cornfields, sunflower fields, thorn trees with nests on their branches, poplars, yuccas in bloom, pampas grass, fields white with fennel in bloom ("capo" they call it here). Many *tobianos* (horses with splotches of brown and white). A partridge on the road. An owl. And a gaucho on horseback.

We arrive in the town of Clara. The church is small, the synagogue is big. Mr. Rosenfeld (60 years old) lives across from the synagogue. He tells us: "Now they build churches; but not synagogues," and "30% of the population is Jewish: 70 Jewish families; about 200 non-Jewish." The synagogue, built in 1914, is similar to the sephardic ones in Israel: painted pink and light blue, with the *bima* (pulpit) in the center and two balconies for the women; mosaic floor. Interesting intersection: San Martín Avenue and Barón Hirsch Street. One hears *yargón* spoken in the street. Yargón (jargon) is Idisch (**yid**-deut**sch**). They were born here but their R is guttural. The children leave.

The cemetery is 3 km away in the open fields. Familiar names: Blinder, Bercovich. Beautiful marble, black, flecked, brown.

We arrive in Sajaroff. This is the town that was called La Capilla when Máximo Yagubsky was born here; the name was changed later to honor Sajaroff, who brought over and implemented the idea of cooperativism. There is a beautiful small synagogue, one floor only, paved with mosaic, and a central place with lovely carved wood.

A gaucho on horseback

Sajaroff synagogue

Blue curtains run on two wires dividing the room into three: L'Chaim hall, temple, school (with blackboard and two wooden benches like the ones in the School of Exact Sciences of the University of Buenos Aires on Perú street). We enter the community services hall. A young Jew, redheaded and freckled, not very communicative, tells us the town has 350 inhabitants, of which 100 are Jews (30%). The *jéder* (school) is a kindergarten (*gan*).

In Villaguay there is a hall but no synagogue. Much sun, very few trees.

Villa Domínguez: It is small, green, shaded. As in Clara, the temple is made of bricks. It has wooden benches for 150 men; space for the women to the side. It's seldom used, says the man who has the key. If there is a *jahrzeit* (first year anniversary of a death) it is difficult to get together a *minyan* (quorum of 10 men necessary for prayers to be … valid? heard?). Clarita retorts: "That's because women are not counted. You should push for it, make them count." In Dominguez we did not see any churches.

Dominguez has 1,500 inhabitants, ca. 500 Jews (30%). We chatted with Mrs. Adela Oyernitzky, Polish, who came to this country when she was seven years old. She has three married children: one in Israel, two in Paraná. Señora Adela tells us she prays, without understanding what she says, from her *tasche* (literally, "pocket"; used to denote the small pocket-sized prayer book).

The parents of Isabel Lvovsky (Livosky) exTaran were from Colonia Clara. She was born in the town of Domínguez.

In San Gregorio, 2 leagues (14 km) away, there is a cemetery that we did not see because to get in one needs to take the key from Villa Dominguez and afterwards return it, and we didn't want to have to go back.

The roads between Clara and Sajaroff, between Villaguay and Villa Dominguez, and between Dominguez and Basavilbaso are dirt — grey, black, brown. Going from Dominguez to Basavilbaso the road runs along the tracks of the narrow-gauge train.

Basavilbaso seems to be as large as Villaguay, but more prosperous, greener. This time it's the synagogue that is on the corner of Avenida San Martín and calle Barón de Hirsch! There is a Banco Institucional Cooperativo (Institutional Cooperative Bank). The synagogue is large; it has two storeys. It's made of cement; ugly. In the front it says: "Tefileh le Moishe." There is a plaque to "Miguel Sajaroff 1873–1958. He dedicated his life to cooperativism and agronomy." Another "to the Agricultural Society of Lucienville on its 75th anniversary, 1900–1975. First agrarian cooperative of the country." The church is smaller than the synagogue.

Basavilbaso belongs to the old Colonia Lucienville. The pharmacist Don Jaime (Chaim) is the one who knows about the town, we were told by the vegetable-store "paisanos" (i.e. Jews) half a block away. Chaim tells us the young people leave, but not as much to the cities as to Israel.

The cemetery of Basavilbaso is about 4 times bigger than Clara's. But they are similar: both about 4 km from town and in the middle of the fields; men buried on one side, women on the other. Only in the last few years a couple of joint tombs were made, for man and wife together. All tombs face East. They have inscriptions in Hebrew (although perhaps some of them are in Idisch) and Spanish, with photos of the deceased.

"Eloísa of the cemetery" has been a cemetry keeper for 40 years. She was brought up by a Jewish family and knows the community very well. Her sister-in-law is in charge of the cemetery at Clara. Eloísa's son is a marble worker and sometimes she goes with him to San Gregorio to set up monuments.

She says "And then came the priest..."

Clarita "The rabbi?"

Eloisa "Yes, that, the rabbi."

Three hundred meters from the cemetery there is an old country house, a synagogue, where Eloisa tells us people go and pray once a year. It makes me think of the wailing wall, with its little isolated room for the women with two tables covered with cloths. Nearby there are long thatch-roofed barns for keeping fowl.

There are many *sulkies* (horse-drawn carts), all over the place. According to Lieberman's book "Tierra soñada" *(Land of our dreams)* the sulkies with 4 wheels are Jewish, i.e. Russian; the ones with 2 wheels are gauchos'.

It seems the two "cities," Villaguay and Basavilbaso, are the urban centers corresponding to the two old colonies, Clara and Lucienville.

In the cemetery of Basavilbaso I find: a Rosa A. de Schuster who was born in 1905 (same year as my mother) and died when she was 34 years old (1939); an Arón Rubinstein who died in1970; a Dujovne; Tobías Tarán (in his youthful photograph he resembles Leonardo); Falicoff.

^j My maternal great-grandfather Baruj Isaac Schuster was born in 1856 (approximately). He arrived in Argentina on the boat El Pampa together with his wife Paulina Rabinovich and their six children, among them my grandmother Rosa, born in 1885. She was almost 6 years old when they came so she must have remembered the boat trip; yet I never heard her mention it. Paulina Rabinovich had two more children before she died, five years after they arrived in Entre Ríos. Isaac marries again and soon thereafter his 8 children from his first marriage leave for Buenos Aires, where they founded the Casa Schuster dealing with footwear.

My grandmother Rosa marries Simón Berlatzky about whom we know very little. Simón died on the operating table, of an intestinal embolism, in 1907. My mother was two years old and her brother Eduardo not yet one. With Rosa widowed, her brother Enrique takes on the role of father to her children. During my childhood, the siblings of my grandmother are an important part of my life. From the second marriage of Baruj Isaac six more children are born, my grandmother's half siblings.

The six Schuster siblings that arrived together from Russia were: Avis (Aba), Adolfo (Wolf), Enrique (Herschl), Rosa (Ipritzaka), Adela (Eidi)

My great-grandparents Baruj and Paulina Schuster with their 8 children
From left to right —
Standing: Pedro, Enrique, Avis, Paulina, Adela, Sara
Sitting: Adolfo, Baruj, Rosa, Elisita
Children: Pablo, Rubén, Fanula

and Sara (Haye). In parentheses are the names with which they were registered in the Immigration office upon arrival. Just like my mother did, I called Rosa's siblings Tío (uncle) or Tía (aunt).

Avis, the older brother, died in 1915 when he was 37. His children Pablo, Fanny and Rubén appear frequently in the family photo album, playing with my mother. Adolfo remained a bachelor and is remembered because he bought a weekend house in San Vicente where the family used to get together and which, years later, was bought from the family by Perón, who used it with Evita.

Rosa, my grandmother, had a son who was born one year after my mother. Named Eduardo Salomón Berlatzky, as a small child he was called Salomoncito but for me he was Tio Eduardo. Eduardo married his first cousin Polly (for Paulina). Polly became an abstract painter and gained a certain recognition. They had two children, my first cousins Hugo and Alicia.

Alicia married Hector Pessah and had two daughters: Verónica and Mariana. Alicia designed and made jewelry for a number of years and then mounted a farm, where she grew organic fruits and vegetables that she distributed to her clients' homes in the city; for several years she had a restaurant on Avenida Santa Fe where the cuisine was based on the products of her farm presented in health-food menus. Alicia, like her mother Polly, smoked a lot and developed lung cancer. She died a few years ago (2003?); the lung cancer had metastasized in her brain and the radiation therapy affected her motor system, so she spent many years incapacitated, in various geriatric homes.

Casa Schuster shoe store in Buenos Aires, established after the 8 childen of Baruj and Paulina Schuster left the Colonias.

My great–grandparents Schuster and their 8 children

Isaac Baruj Schuster + Paulina Rabinovich

Avis +Sofía Poliakov
1. Pablo
2. Fanny
3. Rubén

Enrique + María Berman
1. Paulina
2. Violeta
3. Isidoro
4. Avis

Adela + José Itzcovich
1. Juan
2. Roberto
3. Paulina
  a. Hugo
  b. Alicia
4. Arnolda
  a. Silvia
  b. Horacio

Pedro + Sarita
1. Gusti
2. Gustavo

Adolfo

Rosa + Simón Berlatzky
1. Paulina
  + Abi
    a. Hector
    b. Elsa
2. Eduardo +

Sara + Ernesto Barugel
1. Teté
2. Ester (Pochola)
  + Azulay
    a. José
    b. Hebe
    c. Jorge Ernesto
3. Raul

Elisita + Arturo Barugel

Family tree courtesy of my cousin, Horacio Hirsch

My grandmother Rosa (abuelita) with siblings, spouses and children
From left to right —
Back row: Ernesto and tia Sarita Barugel; Arturo and tia Elisita Barugel;
  tio Eduardo, mami and abuelita; tio Enrique and tia Maria Schuster
Children: Isidoro, Paulinita and Avis Schuster; Pochola and Teté Barugel;
  Violeta Schuster

My mother, Paulina, and her brother, Eduardo

My cousin Hugo, whom I adored as a child and who is five years younger than I am, left Argentina soon after getting a degree in sociology (which was a new career in the University of Buenos Aires). He never returned to Argentina and became estranged from the women in his family, whom he never saw again. In my home Polly was nicknamed "La polilla" (the moth) because she ate up the family ties. In fact, Polly distanced Rosa from her grandchildren Hugo and Alicia, and she was hostile towards my mother for reasons we have not been able to fathom (although we considered all kinds of possibilities with Hugo). Due to this family situation, which anguished Eduardo and my mother, I had virtually no relationship with my cousins until Alicia, already sick, sought to get close — which we did; and Hugo, after the death of Alicia, unexpectedly sent me an e-mail and we reconnected.

^k I have a couple of references to the Barón Hirsch colonies of Brazil:

(i) One is through Saúl Bischle (an acquaintance of my colleague Dale Ingmanson), in whose house in Recife we spent two nights in 1981. The wife of Saúl, Eva Schwatzky, is from a family of colonos of Colonia Philipson. Her family arrived in Porto Alegre in 1895.

(ii) The other is through Clarita Mallar. Her mother was born in Russia. Until age 12 she lived in the colonia Four Brothers (Quatro Irmaos) and after that in Buenos Aires. Clarita's grandmother was feisty: her husband had taken her under false pretenses from the big city (Kiev? Odessa?) to the countryside, where he bought and sold cattle (he did not cultivate the land). Then he took her to Brazil. He took pride in letting people know that he was not a colono but had gone <u>with</u> the colonos to continue buying and selling. This was in Rio Grande do Sul, hot and primitive. "Las mujeres se abichaban por dentro," says Clarita, meaning that women got varmints inside their genitals. This, for good reason, impressed Clarita no end; she dwelt on it time and again.

The grandmother bought magazines and copied the fashionable city fashions, making clothes for the girls that were totally absurd out in the countryside. Forty years later she still criticized Clarita for not dressing up her daughter Graciela in starched dresses, ribbons and bows.

The grandparents went by boat to Buenos Aires, descending the river Paraná. During the trip one of their children died on board and had to be thrown into the river. One year later Clarita told me she had asked an aunt of hers, who said they didn't throw the child into the river but buried him on the banks. A few years ago, an uncle of Clarita's went to Quatro Irmaos and came back saying "they surely did us a favor by not staying there; there is nothing but jungle." The family Matraj is also from Quatro Irmaos.

In Buenos Aires the grandfather died of *carbuncle* (infection) and the grandmother became a widow with 6 children when she was 36 years old. Clarita's mother, who was a girl of 14 at the time, and her 12-year-old sister, went to work packaging milk candies in the Mu Mu factory of the Groisman family (the same factory that was ordered to close down at the time of Perón in the 1940s when the owners refused to make a donation demanded by Evita for one of her causes).

The egyptology connection

How it came to pass that I went to Egypt

By January 1961 my affair with GF had become all-consuming. A resolution — GF or HRR? — was imperative. I had always been very close to my parents and needed to discuss the matter with them. Actually, HRR sent me: "I took you from your parents' home and promised to care for you; I cannot do it now so you should go back to them" (!) But they were not in Buenos Aires: they were in Sudan, in what had been the southern stretches of the Egyptian Empire, excavating a compound and temple of the time of Ramses II at a site called Aksha. So off to Sudan I went.

Not directly. The route was with Alitalia via Rome, to Khartoum. HRR took me to the airport — was it already Kennedy or was it still Idlewild? — and saw me off. Somehow (he often would have me paged when and where I least expected it), GF managed to let me know that he was taking a parallel flight on some other airline and would be meeting me in the Rome airport. So, à la Cary Grant and Audrey Hepburn, we had an incredible 'Roman Holiday' for 3 days before I went off to Khartoum.

We stayed in a hotel named Elizabeth Regina, which appealed because its logo was ER which are/were my initials. We spent all day in the room 'romancing' and ended up starved at 4 pm when all restaurants were closed: this was Italy, and in those days, like in Argentina, the notion of eating outside meal times was non-existent. Eating habits have changed a lot since then … We were there precisely at the time when Lumumba (prime minister of the Democratic Republic of the Congo) was assassinated. The craziness in Congo and the craziness in my personal life seemed to go hand in hand. A reminder of it all when I finally arrived at UCSD was the name of Third College: Lumumba-Zapata…[1]

We were lost to the world, GF and I. Part of our reverie was disappearing altogether without leaving a trace, going off to live in some remote place… It eventually happened: we did leave everything and everybody behind and came to La Jolla. But that january I continued on to Sudan and GF went back to California. His wife, by then, had already left, saying she 'could not compete' with me.

But HRR was not about to give me up. An agreement was struck (how? when?) that I would be left alone during my time communing with my parents, and that neither GF nor HRR would attempt to communicate with me or visit. In fact Aksha was in the middle of nowhere: certainly there were no phones or telegraphs, and letters took forever and had to be picked up in the closest town which was a Nile crossing and several hours cross-desert away.

However, after a month in Sudan, when the excavation season was over, I took the boat down the Nile with my parents to Egypt. And when we arrived in Aswan, there was HRR, come to meet us. So we saw Egypt together: Elephantine, the Valley of Kings, Karnak, and traveled in the exquisite train (à la Orient Express) to Cairo. We climbed Giza — today it seems unreal, but one did it in those days. And we rode camels; mine was called California: prediction of things to come? An omen? Actually we had a lot of fun and laughed a lot trying out our almost non-existing arabic in the street. We were like two kids. We _were_ two kids. That's precisely what the difference was in my relationships. In GF I had met a man; a man with irresistible (to me) allure and sex appeal. As I told my father, I felt like a 'tigre cebado' — a tiger that has been fed human meat and cannot be restrained from it. I had to have GF, to feel him, to touch him, to smell him, to cavort with him.

But I cared deeply for HRR and felt terrible about leaving him. To stay and live with longing forever? Or to leave and live with guilt?

---

[1] I now find out the revolutionary name never was officially approved, Angela Davis and Herbert Marcuse notwithstanding. The College was simply called Third, until in 1993 it became Thurgood Marshall College.

Ah … 'Casablanca.' There is an Elsa (Ilsa, actually) — Ingrid Bergman. But she chooses to stay with her husband and forgo the lover. Was it the morality of Hollywood that made her choose so? Years later, in another iconic (for us) film, 'Hiroshima mon amour' (story by Marguerite Duras), the woman also leaves her lover in spite of the powerful feelings at play, and goes back to her husband. Well … I didn't.

The manner in which it all resolved was, for many years, very difficult for me to even think about. As my grandson Avi — who wants to know — reminds me, GF had written this story into his book of remembrances,[2] but I had him take it out, for it made me uncomfortable. But now both GF and HRR are dead and I can look at it frontally — rather than peek at the situation with squinting eyes, looking peripherally, not really wanting to re-see that street in Manhattan, in front of the Donnell branch of the New York Public Library very near MOMA. GF had flown in from California to force the issue, and he met us (HRR and myself) at that location and told HRR he was taking me to California with him. And there were blows. HRR's glasses fell to the ground. More blows. Then they talked it out. Truly I don't remember much else. In my mind now I see the situation re-created in those nature shows I love to watch on TV: the two males locking horns over possession of the female. Elks. Moose. They don't fight to the death but at some point one of the rivals knows he's beaten and retreats. I must've said something. But what? How? The next thing I know I am on an airplane to California. I took nothing, had only what I was wearing, a black and white corduroy skirt my mother had made me. When we arrived in California, GF took me to a store in downtown San Diego and bought me clothes. Unreal. Including a beautiful pink kerchief of gauze-like material to wear in the little Simca convertible car — that he had brought back from some trip to Europe — so my hair would not fly all over my face. We kept that scarf; it must be in the files where we once placed it with our love letters.

I got carried away by the story and left out a chunk: what happened after Cairo? HRR went back to New York; my parents were continuing

---

2 Called 'Reminiscences and Ruminations,' this book is as yet unpublished.

their travels and I went with them, to Athens and then to Constantinople and to Paris. From Paris I went back to NY. In all those places GF followed me via telephone calls, He was unstoppable. I found out later that in one month he spent 2,000 dollars — which would be close to 20 thousand in today's money.[3]

What was my father doing in Sudan?

In 1959, UNESCO sent out a worldwide appeal for countries to help save 'the treasures of Nubia': the treasures were the monuments from Ancient Egypt that were about to be lost under the waters of the Nile as a consequence of the new dam that was being built in Aswan. My father, Abraham Rosenvasser, was an egyptologist. He was also a lawyer, but by 1959 my brother had taken over the practice and my father could fully devote himself to ancient history. So he took on the UNESCO challenge and got together an archeological expedition that was awarded a couple of sites to excavate in Nubia — the region to the south of Ancient Egypt that is now mostly in Sudan. The excavations took place from november to march — the winter season — three years in a row, mainly 1961, 1962, and 1963. I was there in 1961, from february 15 until the season ended in march.

Aftermath

The agreement with UNESCO was that the archeological missions could keep one-half of the excavated finds. Argentina's portion left Aksha by 'faluca' (sailboat) on the Nile and eventually made it to the port of Buenos Aires where the boxes lingered (two years was it?) until a political maneuver by my father got them out of storage to the basement of the Museum of Natural History of La Plata. With huge resilience, patience, minimal funds, and the dedicated help of his then-graduate-student Perla Fuscaldo, my father managed to mount an exhibit hall showcasing the finds. It opened in 1977.

---

[3] Telephone calls were very expensive in those days. And cumbersome — no direct dialing overseas, everything done through operators. One did not use the phone, which is why I have 30 years of weekly letters to and from my parents while I was in the USA and they were still alive.

About 25 years later I went with friends to visit the exhibition. It turned out the Aksha Hall was closed to the public because the stones were deteriorating. I was very upset that so much effort by my father was being shut off behind closed doors, and offered to look into the matter. The end result was that I co-curated with museum staff a whole new exhibit hall. Renamed Egyptology Hall and properly rehoused among its peer anthropology halls in the upper story of the museum, it opened in 2013.

The Delta and Sinai

All the stories that involve my father are centered in upper Egypt, land of basalt and sandstone. But in the 1990s I had the good fortune of spending time in an argentinian dig in lower Egypt, land of mud and limestone. It was led by my father's former student, Perla Fuscaldo. There are no monuments in these digs, mostly pottery. My extant impression is of a desert strewn with plastic trash that is blown about by constant wind, and where, in spite of the large tracts of sand, we were in a kind of prison, for it is forbidden to walk about,[4] lest one hit a mine left over from the Yom Kippur War of 1973 or from the 6 Days War of 1967. The house where the archeological team lived was in the town of Qantara, right on the Suez Canal. There was a statue there, of soldiers during war with Israel; I think it was Egyptian soldiers recapturing the east coast of Sinai. Whenever a large cargo ship moved along the narrow canal the scene seemed taken from a cheap stage where a flat cardboard cut-out ship slides between two rows of houses. It was so odd that I took a photograph; a policeman immediately came and took the film from my camera — military zone, no pictures allowed.

Perla had the concession to Tell el Ghaba — that is, the Egyptian government's rights to excavate that site. She also worked for many years at another site in the Delta, Tell el-Daba, with the Austrian archeological expedition under the leadership of Manfred Bietak. This

---

4 This reminded me of our daughter Paoli in Antarctica, where she went on a research job: she is an ice and rock climber, and she longed to get out on the ice fields, but found to her consternation that because of ecological fragility they were out of bounds.

was the site of the city of Avaris, capital of the hyksos when they conquered Egypt. And, it seems that is the general area where the hebrew people helped build Pi-Ramses, the Delta capital of Ramses II. This link between my father and Exodus, it seems to me, needs to be preserved in our family lore, so we have integrated it into our storytelling at the yearly celebration of Passover.

And so I travel with Ramses II over the years, accreting my understanding of his times as I meet him again and again. And I wonder about power and the rise and fall of empires, as I did with my father near Luxor, when, in unison, we conjured up Shelley's poem, 'Ozymandias'[5]:

> I met a traveller from an antique land
> Who said: "Two vast and trunkless legs of stone
> Stand in the desert. Near them, on the sand,
> Half sunk a shatter'd visage lies …
> And on the pedestal these words appear:
> My name is Ozymandias, King of Kings;
> Look on my works, ye mighty, and despair!"

Romancing Egypt

My trip in 1961 is part of my personal romance. But the romance of Egypt and the Sudan persists. I did not want to go back there on a trip that GF took with friends in the 1990s because I wanted my memories pristine, unlayered by modern changes. Yet …

GF and I sprinkled our talk with arabic, as expressive and full of connotations to us as spanish: 'maalesh' (or 'lástima') when a point was lost in the tennis court; 'bukra' (as a substitute for 'mañana') when delays were involved; 'nus wa nus' ('mitad mitad') when we were sharing a dish; 'bakshish' (or 'propina') when considering gratuities.

In our patio we have two wooden signs (made by Paoli). One of them points to the canyon, with an arrow; the inscription is 'To Wadi Beta.' It is a take-off on Wadi Halfa (Wadi 'alfa), the name of the nubian town one flew into to go to Aksha. This was the original, the first, or

---

[5] Ozymandias was a greek name for the egyptian pharaoh Ramses II.

alpha, wadi. The wadi in La Jolla is second to the one in Sudan, ergo —
as in the greek alphabet — it is Wadi Beta.

The other wooden patio sign is a picture of a swan with the
inscription: 'Aswan.' It is an indicator that this is a place of peace,
where one goes for prolonged vacations to cure the body and the soul.
Like people did in the 19th century when they had consumption
(tuberculosis): they went to the Cataract Hotel in Aswan and lay on the
chaises longues drinking lemon squash served by the beautiful nubian
waiters, all the while looking at the island of Elephantine on the other
side of the tumbling Nile waters. In our home parlance, one went 'to
the wadi' or 'to Aswan' to get away from it all.

The wonder of this 'egyptology connection' is the refuge it has
afforded in my imagination. It is peopled by pharaohs on the shores of
the Nile, by mideastern armies using Canaan/Palestine as a corridor in
their wars, and by my parents. It offers a space into which I am easily
catapulted and where I can wander. I just stumbled upon an article
about an effort to clear the german landmines in the egyptian desert
that are left over from WWII. This conjures up a 17-year-old GF in his
kibbutz, crouched over a radio that chronicles the advance of Rommel,
the Desert Fox, into El Alamein; and the fear, in his otherwise never
fearful heart, that the Nazis will make it into Palestine.

So this space into which I wander is also inhabited by a GF that
pre-dates our meeting, who has accompanied me in my mental forays
all the years that we were together…

2009 My remembrance of Aksha

Presentation at the Conference in Aswan commemorating 50 years since the UNESCO-sponsored excavations in Nubia

In January 1961, I took some time off from graduate school to join my parents in the excavations in Nubia. My memories of that time are so vivid and rich that I would like to share some of them with you. In re-creating the time, people and place, it is possible I'm not telling you anything very new; excavations in Nubia nowadays may well look and function the same way they did in the early 1960s. However, this account is a very personal remembrance of Aksha, based on my recollections bolstered by the letters of my parents and the photographs taken by my mother.

Let me introduce Professor Rosenvasser: in his tourist garb at Karnak, Baedeker in hand; and in his expeditionary mode, sitting on the head of Mwt, wearing his favorite desert foot-gear — alpargatas, the Argentinian version of rope-soled espadrilles, tied with a piece of string.

Left: Rosenvasser, Baedeker in hand, at Karnak, 1950

Below: Rosenvasser on the head of Mwt, 1950

We lived in the village of Aksha where workers were recruited for the excavations. By the last campaign in 1963 there were very few inhabitants left; they had been resettled in far-off Khasm el-Girba on the Atbara River, more than 1,000 kilometers South of Wadi Halfa.

Our living quarters were in one of the adobe buildings. Outside there was a built-in bench where the locals sat, wrapped up in thick blankets, taking their siesta in the warm sun. The four men that ran our lodgings had been trained by the British during the British Mandate, to be proper and punctilious in their tasks; for example, at table, food was offered on the guest's left and plates were removed from the right side. At table (below) we see Henri de Contenson of the French portion of the mission, smoking his pipe. I am seated to his right. My father and mother sit across from each other on the left and right side of the table respectively. To my mother's right is Kazimir Michalowski. To the right of the server is Marie-Jeanne de Contenson, wife of Henri; she was in charge of the kitchen, menus and so forth. She loved to laugh and sing, and one day had us all making crêpes in the kitchen under her watchful eye.

Sharing a meal in Aksha

Left: My father and mother making crèpes

Below: Sliding down the dunes with my mother

Thursday was payday, and Friday was the day of rest for the workers and the day for going visiting for the members of the archeological missions. The Scandinavians were across the Nile and visits were exchanged between the two missions. The princess Margarethe of Denmark, archeology enthusiast, stayed with the Scandinavians for a while. The archeological mission of the University of Chicago was some distance up the river; the members stayed in well-appointed riverboats. One memorable Friday we went to visit Faras, the site of the Polish mission directed by Kazimir Michalowski.

When the campaign was over, we went to Wadi Halfa and took the boat to Aswan. I wonder if the boat still looks the same as it did then with the pontoons on either side to increase the number of passengers it can take. The Argentinian portion of the finds started its long trip from Aksha to Buenos Aires by faluca and is now exhibited in the Natural History Museum of La Plata. It is the only exhibition in Hispanic America that features an Egyptian collection of substance.

2006   From Ancient Egypt to the Museo de La Plata

Article published in the journal of the Museo de La Plata

The Aksha Hall of the Museo de La Plata, installed in 1977 and presently being restructured, takes us back to the times of Ramses II, 3,300 years ago, and the archeological campaigns led by Abraham Rosenvasser more than 40 years ago. This Egyptian collection might seem out of place among the dinosaurs and the artifacts of andine cultures housed in the Museum. Yet, as we recollect the collection's history, we will see how and why this came to be.

Like most of the objects exhibited in this museum, the ones in the Aksha Hall are the result of the personal work of Argentinian scientists associated with La Plata. Therefore, the exhibition preserves a double legacy: on the one hand, as a museum exhibition should, it establishes the authentic presence of an ancient culture; on the other hand, it exemplifies the human effort of Argentinian scientists that makes this presence possible.

The Franco-Argentinian Mission in Sudan

In 1959, faced with the imminent formation of a great artificial lake on the river Nile caused by the Aswan dam that was then being built in Egypt, UNESCO made a worldwide call for assistance. The call was directed to archeological missions, requesting help in order to rescue the ancient monuments and objects from the valley of the Nile that would otherwise be flooded south of Aswan, in the Egyptian, or Lower, Nubia, and the Sudanese, or Upper, Nubia. The response in Argentina came from the Egyptologist Abraham Rosenvasser, my father, who joined forces with Jean Vercoutter, professor at the University of Lille; together they formed a Franco-Argentinian Mission to excavate the site known as Aksha, where lay the remains of a temple of Ramses II. (Ramses II, of the XIXth dynasty, reigned between 1292 and 1225 BCE). The efforts of Rosenvasser were supported by the CONICET (National Research Council) and the University of La Plata, where he was a member of the faculty.[1] In France the Mission was supported by the Ministry of Foreign Affairs. The association of the two countries was essential for the project to proceed since both were in need of sharing expenses and specialized personnel.

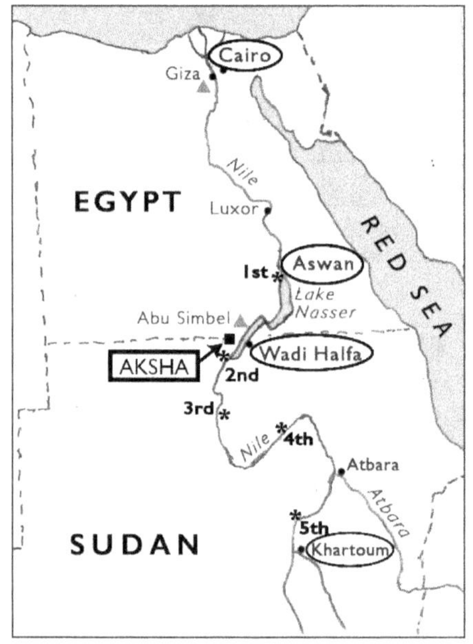

Locations of places mentioned in the text. The numbers indicate the successive cataracts of the Nile.

The agreement of Egypt and Sudan with UNESCO stipulated that the archeological missions could take with them one-half of the excavated pieces. This is how 300 Egyptian pieces from the temple complex and outlying cemeteries arrived in Argentina in the 1960s. This collection is unique in South America; its intrinsic value becomes incalculable

---

[1] He was also Professor of Ancient History I (Orient) in the Facultad de Filosofía y Letras (School of Humanities) of the University of Buenos Aires. His relationship with La Plata was long-standing: He had taught in the High School associated with the University from 1923 to 1942 and was Dean of the School of Humanities in 1957–58 (after the downfall of Perón). In the University of La Plata he was faculty member from 1939 until 1946 (when he was dismissed during Perón's regime) and then from 1956 until 1963.

when we consider that it is no longer possible to take out antiquities from their countries of origin. (Nowadays we are usually faced with the reverse: It is a common occurrence that museums are requested to return pieces from older collections.)

In January 1961 I had the good fortune of visiting my parents in Aksha during the first excavation season (there were three) of the Franco-Argentinian Mission. At the time I was a graduate student at Columbia University. I flew from New York via Rome to Khartoum where I had to wait several hours for the connecting flight to Wadi Halfa, which would take me back again 500 miles to the North. Staff from the airport placed a canvas reclining chair for me next to the runways, so that I might rest under the bougainvillea, watching the planes and the passengers coming and going on foot on the tarmac. From this semi-idyllic setting I went on to a small plane with just a few passengers, and a tall, good-looking Nubian steward dressed in the British Colonial style uniform with shorts and knee-high socks (similar to that worn by policemen in Wadi Halfa).

Policeman
in Wadi Halfa

My parents met me in Wadi Halfa and we went further North, through the desert and across the Nile, to Aksha. The crossing of the desert by car is impressive for there is no road, not even tracks; the driver (hopefully) knows where the ground is firm and in what direction he must aim. The Nile is crossed in *falucas*, small sailboats of ancient design, like the one that is about to cross over the pieces excavated in Aksha, packed in crates, for the first step of their journey to La Plata (see photo).

Faluca loading excavated pieces

Wadi Halfa was a nice town, full of life, the end point of the journey by boat from Lower Egypt (and, conversely, the starting point of the journey down the Nile; below is the boat we took when the digging season was over).

Sailing between Wadi Halfa and Aswan (the side pontoons are add-ons to accommodate passengers traveling in second and third class)

During the months of the excavations (December until March), the members of the archeological Mission went to Wadi Halfa as if to the big city, seeking diversion and a change in scenery. However, even if picturesque, Wadi Halfa was not exactly an entertainment center.

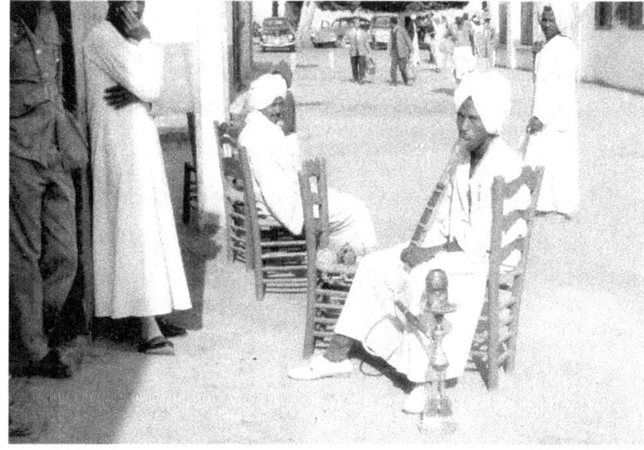

Smoking a narguile
in Wadi Halfa

It is now forty years since that Wadi Halfa disappeared under the waters of Lake Nasser (formed by the Aswan dam). It was the second city in Sudan, with 10,000 inhabitants that were re-settled in other places and have paid the price of this displacement: People who used to grow oranges and sugar cane have had to change their life-style completely and become fishermen. The place nowadays called Wadi Halfa in not the one we knew; it simply bears the same name.

The excavation team and life in Aksha

Who made up the excavation team in Aksha? The members of the Argentinian team included: one historian/epigrapher, my father, in charge of the reading and interpretation of the inscriptions; an architect

Rosenvasser doing
epigraphy

in charge of drawing the plans of the site showing the placement of the finds (one year it was Sergio Domicelj, another year A. Hernandez); and an archeologist (one year, Alberto Rex Gonzalez; another, Pablo Krapovickas). The French team included the archeologist and photographer André Vila — a fun guy, full of anecdotes about the Berbers with whom he had lived for a while; Henri de Contenson, expert in archeology of the Christian era, and the director Jean Vercoutter, whom I never met because he was not in Aksha during my stay there.

The members of the Mission lived in an adobe house, rented from the local inhabitants. Like all the houses of the village, it was in the shape of a long rectangle without windows, oriented so as to minimize the ravages of the sand storms that blow without mercy every now and then. Light came in through doors that opened onto the inside courtyard. The roof was made of palm fronds. The houses were the same color as the sand of the desert. One would think they had been designed with a modern criterion of ecological architecture where houses blend in with the surrounding landscape. The Mission's house lodged the members of the team in individual rooms; there was also a dining room, a bathroom (I've totally forgotten how it was equipped), and a kitchen.

The local people wore cotton tunics: white for the men, black for the women. The men also wore white turbans. Curiously (for us) they lay down to take a nap at noon in the sun on adobe benches abutted to the house, wrapped from head to toes in thick wool blankets. For them, we must realize, it was winter.

Nubian houses

The cook and the butler, Mohammed and Ahmed, were Nubians who had been trained by the English during the British Mandate in Sudan. Therefore, very correct and well mannered, they served food on the left of each seated diner and withdrew dishes from the right. Fortunately, the wife of Contenson was in charge of the kitchen, so the cuisine was French rather than English. At teatime, mounds of halva (a sweet made from sesame seed) were served, that we ate as if there were no tomorrow.

Fridays were visiting days when the members of the various archeological missions in the region visited each other's excavations. So it was that one Friday the Scandinavians from the other side of the Nile came for tea. Another time it was the Spaniards. On another occasion, the Poles from Faras, famous for the director of its Mission (Michalovsky) and the frescoes of the Christian churches found there. On another Friday we visited them.

Thursday was payday for the workers. The foreman, seated next to Rosenvasser or other responsible member of the Mission, in a hut made of palm fronds, gave out the money and kept track of payments in the book of records. Rosenvasser and the older members of the team spoke enough Arabic to communicate with the foreman and the domestic help, whose English was, at best, rudimentary.

The ritual of payday

Every day, after the Mission women's ritual sunbath in the dunes (in those days it was fashionable to be sunburned and we knew nothing about skin cancer), I went by the place where my father, notebook in hand, copied hieroglyphs, interpreted and translated them.[2] At those times he showed me things of interest. For example the great Western wall of temple's courtyard where, to the North of the doorway is the relief representation of Asiatic people. On the other side of the doorway, the South side, are portrayed the Kushites, with their characteristic negroid traits. It is an impressive representation of the vanquished peoples of the North and the South. These stones have remained in the museum in Khartoum but the drawings are reproduced in Aksha Hall.

Rosenvasser translating hieroglyphs

My mother, among other things, was in charge of the inventory of the pieces that were being lined up under the palm trees. She painted with black paint an identifying number (still visible in many of the pieces in the exhibition) and a register was made, using the ubiquitous

---

[2] Part of the interpretation work involved looking for parallels between the inscription at hand and known inscriptions conveying similar invocations in other temples (such as Karnak and Abydos).

portable Olivetti (typewriter), that included a description of the piece and the spot where it was found. I was her helper. We took very seriously the admonishment to avoid turning over the stones by putting our hands underneath since Nubian scorpion bites are deadly.

The officers of the Antiquities Service of the Sudanese government came often to monitor the excavations. They were friendly but strict. Their inspection was to ensure that all objects found were rigorously inventoried (especially the small finds, such as amulets, statuettes or rings) and that nothing left the country without having been strictly controlled.

There were, also, some exotic elements in this archeological mission, such as the policeman and the itinerant salesman riding camels, or the water carrier with his burro.

A traveling salesman on his camel

A water carrier with his burro

History of the site and excavations

Aksha is situated in what is nowadays the Republic of Sudan. In the time of the Pharaonic Empire of Ramses II and his father Seti I, this region was part of Egyptian Nubia. It is located on the Western bank of the river Nile, on the Tropic of Cancer, somewhat to the North of the Second Cataract and a few kilometers South of Abu Simbel (the most famous of the temples of Ramses II, that was cut from the rock in which it was hewn, lifted 60 meters on the cliff, and relocated, to avoid the waters from the Aswan dam).

In the days of glory of the Empire, the domains of Pharaoh extended from the Mediterranean Sea to the Fourth Cataract, about four hundred kilometers to the South of Aksha. Pharaoh showed his power by establishing settlements. One of these was Aksha, with its temple and small surrounding city.

The ruins of Aksha are already mentioned by travelers in 1813 and several more times thereafter during the XIXth century. In 1906, the first photographs of the site were taken by Breasted, well-known historian from the University of Chicago (his book, cited in the bibliography, is a classic). By the time the Franco-Argentinian Mission arrived, a good portion of what had been seen before had disappeared: The people of the area had made use of the Egyptian temple and the basilica that the Christians had built on top of it, to build their houses and their *saakias* with the stones, and to fertilize their fields with the adobe.

The temple excavated by the Franco-Argentinian mission had the classical structure: a semi-public portion consisting of the entry pylon and a courtyard with portals supported by pillars, and a private portion (open only to priests) consisting of a hall and a three-part sanctuary. Outside the temple were found seven deposits with the names of Ramses II and Seti I in their stone entryways. Other structures excavated were the granaries, the living quarters of the clergy, the palace of the governor (in the exhibition there is a monumental door jamb with inscriptions belonging to this palace) and, further away, the area where the common people lived. Towards the Nile the pier was found and excavated. We know, from drawings of that time, that the boats that moored on this pier were identical to the falucas of today.

A faluca on the Nile viewed from the pier at the excavation site

In a neighboring site named Bedier, a tomb belonging to an Egyptian official that pre-dated Seti and Ramses was excavated by the Franco-Argentinian Mission. The objects found in there (bowls, jugs, etc.) are part of the collection of the Museo de La Plata. Furthermore, three cemeteries were found: two of them belonging to Nubian cultures prior to the Empire, and a third one from Meroitic times. Originating in Meroe, a town South of Nubia, this important culture post-dates Ramses; its remains include monuments and pyramids that are less well known than those of Egypt.

We have looked at three layers of remains in Aksha: the old Nubian cultures, the Egyptian and the Meroitic. A fourth layer, the most recent, is the Christian culture. The church photographed by Breasted in 1906 was built with adobe bricks, as is characteristic of places inhabited by different successive cultures, but also with stones from the Egyptian structures. In the Museo de La Plata's collection there is a capital from a column belonging to this church, a gargoyle and some potsherds.

From Aksha to La Plata

Some of the excavated stones turned out to be in too bad a condition to be moved and they remained in situ. Others traveled to Khartoum. Some were sent from there to France. Others to Argentina, where they remained for over ten years in their packing boxes until it was agreed to exhibit them in their present location in the Museum's ground floor. In fact, given the thematic distribution of materials in the Museum, the Aksha collection should have been housed on the top floor together with the other collections of anthropology and archeology. At the time this was not done because there were doubts as to whether that floor would withstand the weight of the Egyptian materials.

The exhibition opened in 1977, curated by Rosenvasser and his then-student Perla Fuscaldo.[3] Mounted with the resources and know-how of that time, the exhibition hall was painted black (ceiling and walls), portals were erected using original jambs and lintels completed with reconstructions, the stones were covered with a protective resin, and photographs and copy were produced which resulted in an extremely well documented exhibition. Unfortunately, continuing deterioration of the stones together with vandalism by some visitors, resulted in Aksha Hall being closed to the public for the last several years, and opened only by special request. It was speculated that the stones' deterioration was due to the high ambient humidity of La Plata, and the rudimentary mounting of the pieces to the walls with cement and iron brackets (that rust). It was believed (indeed, it became a museum myth) that in order to stop the deterioration it would be necessary to install (and maintain) a climate-control system, something that would be extremely hard to do.

Now, thirty years later, thanks to a grant from the Paul Getty Foundation, we have been able to bring from the USA an expert in

---

[3] Fuscaldo is Professor of Ancient Orient in the University of Buenos Aires, and researcher of the CONICET (National Research Council). She has been Director of the Argentinian Archeological Mission at Tell el-Ghaba in the Sinai peninsula. She participates in the Austrian excavations at Tell el-Dab'a in the Nile delta. Moreover, she is engaged in the study of the ceramics (there are more than 200) of the Aksha collection and is an active participant in the renovation of the Aksha Hall.

conservation to consult on the state of the stones and formulate plans to recondition and conserve them. This is how we found out that the "protective" resin is the biggest problem, because with the passage of time it peels off, taking with it grains of sand from the stone; that is to say, instead of protecting, it disintegrates the stone. Therefore the first step, which is being carried out now, is to remove with infinite care the covering resin. The work of the excellent team in charge of this process has been well documented by S. Campos in the newspaper Clarín (cited in the bibliography). After this, the other problem to be addressed is the efflorescence of the salts that form white deposits on the surface of the stones. Finally, when the design for the new exhibition is developed, modern methods that are stable and reversible will be sought to remount the pieces. There is much to be done.

In his address on the occasion of the inauguration of the Aksha Hall, Rosenvasser said: "As we inaugurate [the exhibition] today, I can only formulate my vehement wish that the University shall endeavor, by all possible means within its purview, to secure its proper presentation and adequate conservation so that the important educational purposes inherent in the exhibition shall be maintained for the good of the entire Nation." His wish is coming true.

Some whys and wherefores

Rex Gonzalez, past director of the department of archeology of this Museum, participated in one of the three campaigns to Nubia. In an interview with the newspaper Noticias (pg. 66–68) published on April 14, 2005, he said: "I had to excavate a Meroitic temple [sic] from the beginnings of the Christian era and everything we found was already known. It's more important to work in Catamarca, La Rioja..." Clearly, the notion of what is and isn't important is very personal, and what drives one man of science is not necessarily what drives another.

But the question persists: Why did Rosenvasser, who lived in Argentina, who went to Egypt for the first time in his life when he was more than 50 years old ... Why did he devote himself with such passion to uncovering Egyptian stones and deciphering hieroglyphs? It is our conjecture that Rosenvasser, a liberal agnostic like so many intellectuals of the beginnings of the XXth century, transmuted the traditions lived in his childhood in the colony of Jewish immigrants near Carlos Casares, into his quasi-lay interest in the origins of monotheism. The relationships between Egypt and Israel in the time of the biblical Exodus take him along the path of egyptology. And then in 1923 the world resonates with the news of the discovery of the tomb of Tutenkhamen. From my father's library, I still have the issues of the journal The London Illustrated News of that time, with pages and pages of photographs of the mortuary chambers and the treasures lying in there, and the Englishmen Lord Carnarvon and Carter who opened the tomb. Rosenvasser was twenty-five years old. How could he not be enthralled? These circumstances, we believe, give clues to — even if not actual explanations of — the intellectual pursuits of Rosenvasser.

Egyptian profiles: Rosenvasser
in front of a bas-relief

And finally, how come the daughter of Rosenvasser is involved in the process of conservation of Egyptian pieces, and presumes to add her grain of sand to the new, modern presentation of the Aksha Hall? As a young woman I studied physics in the University of Buenos Aires, driven by fascination with the cutting edge discipline that, in those days, fueled imaginations. Physics in the 1950s, one could say, was the equivalent of egyptology in the 1920s. Also, my father knew virtually nothing about physics; and since I lived with my parents and could not take physical distance, as young people do today, I had to opt for intellectual distance. Eventually, I ended up directing a science museum in the USA, where I live, creating interactive exhibitions directed at the popular understanding and appreciation of our scientific legacy. And when all is said and done, going from the scientific to the egyptological legacy … well, it's just a question of subject matter!

Bibliography

J.H. Breasted, *A History of Egypt*. Bantam Books, New York. 1967. (original edition, Scribner, New York. 1905)

A. Rosenvasser, "La excavación de Aksha: tres campañas arqueológicas en la Nubia," *Ciencia e Investigación,* Noviembre 1964, Tomo 20, No. 11, pgs. 482–511.

S. Campos, "Restauran en el Museo de La Plata una colección única de piezas egipcias," diario *Clarín,* domingo 16 de abril, 2006.

My Patagonia

Keep those endorphins flowing! It's the mantra for well-being. So: do I love the mountains because they make me feel so well? Or do they make me feel so well because I love them? Impossible to tell. But all that matters is that I love the mountains. And I've gone there again and again throughout my life. Our daughter Paoli has chosen to live in the mountains — in Bozeman, Montana. I, too, contemplated living in the mountains when I was in my mid-twenties: having finished university studies, I was offered a position at the Physics Institute in Bariloche. I seriously considered it, because of the location. But I was too much of a city girl — at that time anyway. The incessant social life and cultural offerings of Buenos Aires appealed too much.

I translate. *November 1953: In my room I've hung one photo of the Everest and two of the Fitz Roy; also one of Einstein with Oppenheimer. It's what I like best of all that is on the walls, because it symbolizes the Facultad and the mountain — the two things that have become essential in my life. Music should also appear, but at the moment I'm somewhat distant from it.*

Mountains beyond the Andes

I never made it to the Everest — in truth, I never tried — but I did go trekking in Nepal's wondrous Langtang valley. This story, as well as others of climbing, hiking, and skiing in the European Alps, in the Southern Alps of New Zealand, in the Sierra Nevada and the Rockies belong in another weft. Because these mountains beyond the Andes are not 'mine,' they were not part of my backyard the way the Patagonian Andes have always felt. So this story is about 'my' mountains, 'my' Patagonia.

Patagonia in the 1940s

I can trace my affair with the mountains to a couple of adventurous trips I took with my parents and brother when I was 10 and 11 years old (1942–43). The northern portion of Patagonia was pretty much a wilderness in those days; few people ventured there. But my father was intrepid, and he organized these voyages with another intrepid family, good friends of ours who travelled in their own car (since going alone in our 1938 Chevy was not a wise option). The itineraries were devised with the help of the Auto Club: booklets were printed specially for us, with a map for each day of the trip; I still have portions of these.

Our car was equipped with books and tin cans of food in a compartment under the rear seat. (I particularly remember the tins of quince jam and sweet potato jam because they were flat and enormous: perhaps 8 by 11 inches; such tins, emptied and filled with an agar mix, were used by my brother and his friends during their high school days for dittoing pamphlets.) The space between the rear seat and the front was large enough to fit a small refrigerator: a made-to-order wooden box lined with cork insulation for the ice (which was bought from an ice-man and came shaped like huge bricks). I could sit and stretch my legs over the top of the icebox. Was I so little? My brother was already tall and when the car hit the first holes in the road, he bounced and hit his head hard on the roof of the car; so we went to a repair shop and had the suspension taken out of the seats to avoid further accidents. The ride was hard but safe. On top of the car we carried the tent, a very large one for the whole family, made of thick canvas; it was extremely heavy.

The roads we took (nowadays there is a highway) went across ranches; there were stretches that were one big mudhole; there were creeks to be traversed that could become roaring water barriers. On one of these crossings the motor got wet and died. The water was rising at an alarming rate, as it does in the afternoons in creeks fed from mountain snow-melt when the sun has been out all day. We got out of the car while we could still open the doors. Someone went to get help and came back with a ranch hand and a pair of young bulls. The yoked bulls pulled and strained but could not budge the car. The water kept mounting. The ranch hand went away and came back with a yoke of mature oxen. They pulled and strained and did get the car out of the creek. When we opened the compartment under the rear seat, the books — all our reading material for the trip — were a pulpy mess.

A side objective of the excursion was attempting to find a cure for my mother's problem with recurring facial boils. We called them furuncles; nowadays they might be considered a form of acne perhaps. In those days it was fashionable for women to wear hats; hats with veils that hid the unsightly furuncles is how my mother weathered social outings. This was before antibiotics. It was said the mud from thermal stations could help. So we included a trip to Copahue, which at that time was a very primitive thermal station in the Andes. The days in Copahue were magical, full of surprises, despite the constant, over-whelming smell of sulphur. The mud ponds and spouts were all over; you had to walk with great care not to get burnt because the wooden paths were few and scattered. The different sources had different prop-erties and different temperatures. I was particularly taken with one that spouted water just below boiling point and therefore was used by everybody for their mate. (mate: the typical southern south american tea drink). Copahue boasts a volcano with a hot lake in its crater. Along its sides are paths the locals use to shuttle between Argentina and Chile. The adults in our group who did this trip, climbing this volcano on horseback, were terrified: the paths are narrow and drop steeply down the sides of the volcano. But the locals handled it casually: men who went over to Chile and got drunk, came back strapped to their horses. Without any guidance from the riders, the horses got them home safely.

In Chile, we climbed the Villarica volcano. There were patches of snow still in january, and we wore snow shoes. But it was in San Martín de los Andes, next to the Lago Lacar, that I first remember looking up wistfully at the top of a mountain and longing to climb it. Just because it was there.

Patagonia in the 1950s

Learning to ski and climb. I was 18 when I took my first trip to Europe (1951). To France, to be precise; with a group from the Alliance Française. By boat. I had never yet been on an airplane; not unusual at the time. Michel, a young guide I met on the tour took me skiing in Barèges (near Pau, close to Bordeaux, where he was from). I had never been on skis before; the method of instruction consisted of letting me go down the hill as best I could, which turned out to be mostly on the seat of my (borrowed) pants. At lunchtime we met on the top of the mountain and had baguette with salami and wine. The empty bottle of wine (I'm not really sure it was the same one, but it makes for a nice story) at night was filled with hot water to keep my feet warm.

It was all very romantic and back in Buenos Aires I sang 'À Paris' and 'Gamin de Paris' and 'Feuilles mortes' wistfully for a couple of months till I shaped up and started studies at the university. Since many of my courses were taken jointly with students of engineering, I befriended several of them. They invited me to go with them to Escobar, on the outskirts of the city, where they practiced mountain-climbing skills in an old abandoned factory. I was amazed that people climbed buildings in order to train for climbing mountains. I myself climbed trees in our backyard: the branches of our jacaranda provided a niche for reading in splendid isolation. The invitation was enticing so I went. We put our bicycles on the train and cycled the last stretch. At the deserted roofless factory we roped up, used holds in the bricks to get to the first story window-holes — the second story when I got good at it — and then rappelled down. It was before the age of nylon, so the ropes were hemp, thick and heavy; they burnt hands and thighs easily when they slipped through; harnesses had not yet been introduced.

The factory-climbing group formed a club, the Club Andino Buenos Aires (CABA). I joined. We often spent the night in the fields near the factory; sleeping bags, no tents. For the return to the city we sometimes went down to the nearby river, the Lujan that flows into the huge Paraná Delta, where we would flag down a public launch, put our bikes in and go down the river (instead of bicycling) to the train station terminal (Tigre).

In winter 1952 a group of us from CABA went skiing in Bariloche. It was my first ski trip after the Pyrenees. We stayed at the lodge of the Club Andino Bariloche (CAB) in Cerro Catedral. It was dorm style and we bought and cooked our own food. None of us knew how to ski (my french experience didn't amount to much) but we had with us a recent austrian immigrant who spoke no spanish but who skied like the gods. Watzl was his name. He taught us by bellowing out instructions: 'schneepflug' was 'snowplough,' 'tzok tzok' meant 'hurry up' or 'faster;' 'immer parallel,' calling for 'christiania' or 'parallel skiing' was only a gleam of hope. Our skis were long (up to the palm of the hand of an outstretched arm overhead), made of oak wood; the bindings had a spring in the back that fit our summer hiking boots which doubled as ski boots. I loved every second of the trip. *Life is glorious, marvelous; hurray! Impossible to be any happier.* And later, *One can only be boundlessly happy here.*

Bariloche's Cerro Catedral is now a large ski resort, with gondolas, an array of runs, modern hotels. It is frequented by argentinians and tourists. But in the 1950s argentinians did not ski — with the exception of the high socio-economic echelon who learnt and did the season in Europe. Nor, for that matter, did they mountain climb or trek or backpack. But the CABA members were almost all european-born or had european parents. They were french, belgian, hungarian, austrian, german, swiss. Most of them had european equipment, which I borrowed for this first excursion. Argentina had no market for such equipment, hence it was simply not available. Which brings me to my next story.

Summers with the French Guides. One of the CABA members, Jacqueline — who later married our ski instructor Watzl and is now, with me, one of only two survivors from those days — invited me to join her group of Guides, the french equivalent of Girl Scouts for young adults. When I was small, my brother had been an active Boy Scout, and I so wished I could go camping and do all the neat stuff my brother did with his troop. But there was no Girl Scouts organization in Argentina. So Jacqueline's invitation was a dream come true.

Before my first big outing with the Guides, the whole troop engaged in making the equipment. Using european models we made our own tents, anoraks, sleeping bags, and backpacks. Our mothers had sewing machines. We used parachute material for the anoraks. For the backpacks we used duck cloth; and then we sent them to an iron-monger for the inner frame and to a shoe-repair man for the leather shoulder straps. Stuffing the down feathers into the sleeping bags was a happy, communal affair; we wore kerchiefs to keep the down out of our hair and probably sang and made merry. I still have the anorak and the sleeping bag; I regret that at some point I gave away my historic backpack. I just remember that looking at it in later years I thought it was so small: we must have carried very, very little. We did not, for instance, have an insulation pad to place under the sleeping bag, just a plastic drop cloth; it was often quite cold, so during those trips I did not menstruate at all, even though usually my period was very regular. And yet we all took with us a skirt, for in the towns we never wore pants.

The trips with the Guides were month-long affairs in the summer: about a dozen of us, mostly from the french school so we spoke french and sang french songs. We traveled to Bariloche as one did then, by train, two nights; sleeping in our bags on top of, or under, the wooden seats in second class. Further south, to Esquel, the train was narrow-gauge and had a wood stove in the middle of the compartment, where we cooked our food. This train has now been turned into a tourist attraction.

In my journals I find an interesting reference to these trips. It's a conversation I'm having with a serious boyfriend at the time, Tito Sirlin, a physicist, who soon thereafter came to the USA and is now at NYU. I translate: *January 1954. "Yesterday I got a call from Pablo. He is going by car with Susana to Mar del Plata* (a large seaside resort about 400 km from Buenos Aires). *They want us to go with them." "I'm certain I won't be allowed to go." "They let you go for two months to the mountains by yourself and you cannot come for 5 days to Mar del Plata?" "It's very different…"*

A few days later: *As mom and pop said: "Why let yourself be talked about? The company you keep is very important and you know Susana's reputation."*

In short: unlike travelling with a boyfriend, going with a group of young women, unescorted, to the mountains, backpacking and camping, was socially uncharted territory and carried no sanctions. There were no precedents. It was actually pretty forward-thinking of my parents to let me go.

An instance that stands out from these trips is an ice traverse we did. The account is written up in the log books of mountain guide Otto Meiling; I found and reread it 50 years later when I visited him in his lodge a couple of years before he died. The group of Guides had climbed to the hut of the Tronador, an iconic mountain that spans the Andes and has three peaks, appropriately called Argentino, Chileno, and Internacional in the center. Four of us had contracted with Meiling to do the traverse to Chile. Meiling was even then a legend in the land: a hardcore european mountain man (bavarian), he had arrived in Argentina early on (1920s) and helped develop Bariloche into a mountaineer's dream; one of the hills bears his name, Cerro Otto, and there he built a lodge and taught skiing.

The day of our traverse, Meiling arrived at the hut of the Tronador with his leather rucksack and ice-axes for us; he said there would be a total lunar eclipse that night and we would take advantage of the light of the full moon to do our traverse, taking a rest during the time of the eclipse. And that is exactly what we did. The Guides had crampons: one of our earlier excursions had been to climb a glacier further south across the Lago Puelo. So, with crampons and an ice axe each, we roped up: Jacqueline, the two Rusconi sisters, myself, and Meiling. We practiced self-arrest techniques and off we went into the moonlight, the icy snow crunching with our steps. During the eclipse we rested in a boulder patch. The next morning we passed border control and took a motor-launch to cross the lake back to town. (It just occurred to me to look up Otto Meiling in Google and I see that the hut in the Tronador was actually built by Meiling himself and nowadays is called Refugio Otto Meiling.)

The Rusconi sisters remained my friends for life (they are both gone now). Vanna ended up living in Bariloche, where we met several times, including once when her sister Renata and I visited: I had been summoned to act as moderator between the two sisters, who wanted to see each other but whose italian tempers would flare up and make it hard to be together. Renata went to live in Italy, and over the years we took many memorable trips together. I would fly to Milan, spend a few days with her (getting over jet lag, brushing up my italian), and then we'd take off to explore Rome or the country around Bologna, to hike in the Dolomites or trek a chunk of the Camino de Santiago.

One other Guide remained a close friend: Marta Brenner, who is now in assisted living, suffering from dementia. Life dealt Marta a raw deal. She had two sons and during their young days, with her husband (a biochemist), the four of them led an adventurous life, canoeing their inflatable boat among icebergs in glacier-fed lakes, camping in South Africa while lions circled their tent, and other pretty fantastic odysseys. Her older son did scuba-diving, hunting for specimens for his father's research, and died during one of his dives. Her younger son was a first-rate mountain climber who died running the rapids in a kayak in the Rio de las Vueltas at the foot of the Fitz Roy massif. Both were very young.

Winter adventures. During the winter 1952 ski trip with the CABA, Watzl (with Frank, Victor, and Ernesto) wanted to do a winter climb of the Needles of the Cerro Catedral. The south side of the Torre Principal had not been done in winter and the CAB had commissioned Watzl to attempt it. Betty Perenyi and I were going with them although we would not climb. The six of us set out with backpacks holding all the equipment, and seal-skins on our skis for the climb up the slope. We (Watzl excepted) were not very good on skis. When one of us fell and could not get up with the heavy backpack, someone would ease near and pull the fallen skier up by the straps of the backpack. When the undulating terrain called for going down the slope, and the skis did not glide very well, we stopped to take off the seal skins from the skis. Then, to go up-hill again, the skins went on again. We got to the ridge near the Torre and set up camp in the snow; one big tent for the men, a small one — that leaked — for Betty and me. A bivouac at 2,500 meters (7,500 feet)! It was so cold, we sat on each others' feet to warm them up; in the morning there was ice in our shoes; we thawed them out using the heat from the alcohol burners (our stoves). Unfortunately the weather turned bad: it was snowing, the wind was fierce and the fog was dense. So we broke camp, took off the seal-skins and skied down the mountain, falling a lot, being lifted a lot. What an adventure! The next day I wrote a poem dealing with the trials and joys of the excursion.

In the winter of july 1953, always short on funds, the CABA leaders secured a barracks on the Cerro Catedral that belonged to the army ski patrol, for a group of us to stay at and go skiing. It was not in the valley where the tourist lodges were, but a quarter of the way up the mountain. Just getting there was a schlep since there were no lifts of any kind. To do a downhill run one first needed to ski down to the valley in order to catch the gondola. At the end of the day one could look forward to the schlep back home to the barracks. But we were a happy group. The bunks were stacked four high. All one's personal stuff was strewn

From a letter to my parents, july 1952. The rhythm is borrowed from Antonio Machado:
Fue una larga noche de tanta agonía!/Afuera el viento barría la nieve sin tregua./Adentro, llovía./Vueltas y más vueltas en la carpa daba;/por qué exponerse a un reuma, pensaba?/a qué tanta legua con foca cinché?/y un rucksack pesado, bajo un sol de estío,/con tanta bravura, en skis, arrastré?/Sacramento!/Oyes tu el viento?/Charlemos aún./Oh! Guantes mojados, Vascolets aguados,/zapatos helados, delicias del ski;/bivouac en montaña! te amo con saña,/no guardas secretos tu ya para mí.

around one's bunk. And if your bunk was the fourth one up, well: happy climbing — and happy descending when you needed to use the outdoor facilities at night.

The summer school of physics. The summer-long school of physics in 1955 was an experience that stands out. At the university we had one good physics teacher, J.A. Balseiro, who had neither resigned nor been ousted by Perón's political regime. He had the idea of starting a physics institute in Bariloche, far from the political turmoil of the big cities. To showcase his idea he organized a summer school in physics at an army site in Bariloche where he envisaged the institute would eventually function. Fast-forwarding to today: the institute was, indeed, founded; it now bears the name Instituto Balseiro; it has university rank and an outstanding reputation for producing first-rate professionals. The story of the origins of the Institute starts with the announcement in 1951 by President Perón that Argentina had developed a new way of producing atomic energy, a startling revelation that received world-wide attention. The implication was that thermonuclear fusion had been produced, a precursor of the hydrogen bomb. The scientist responsible for this achievement was Ronald Richter, an austrian who had worked in Berlin, arrived in Argentina in 1948, and immediately convinced Perón of the viability of his proposed work. Not a single bona fide argentinian scientist was involved in this most secret of projects. Richter set up shop on an island in Bariloche, on the magnificent lake LlaoLlao, eventually moving to the army quarters just across the water. When Richter's claims were debunked, the site — known as the Planta Atómica at that time — was put to use by the incipient project of Balseiro.

I was one of the students in the summer program. There were perhaps two dozen students and half a dozen faculty, several of them from Germany. A variety of courses were given, oriented towards the research interests of the faculty. A wonderful italian physicist, Manlo Abele, introduced us to the propagation of electromagnetic waves in waveguides, a topic I would come back to, years later, when I did my PhD thesis using microwave radiation. Teacher-student relations were close. They included competitive ping-pong games after dinner and outings — horseback riding and trekking in the mountains — on the weekends. I experienced those two months as an idyll; a community of scientists living, working, learning, playing together day in and day out, in a paradise of lakes and mountains. It couldn't be further from the urban setting of the university in Buenos Aires. It seemed so european to me; and indeed it was when I compare it to the École in Les Houches, near Chamonix, where we spent some time in 1969, when GF taught a course there.

The summer of 1955, that was when I got to do most of the trekking routes in the area. To the Laguna Jakob we went with my italian roommate Lucia Lagatta, and two Italians who worked in the Planta Atómica, Mario and Ferruccio. Lucia had no mountain experience, and coming down the scree on the far side of the Cerro Catedral almost paralyzed her with fear, but the two guys took her by the hand and she made it down. Fast-forward: Lucia became a nuclear physicist, had the chance to go on a fellowship to England, where she had a nervous breakdown, was shipped back to Argentina, and never really recovered; she was given an assistantship job at the university in Buenos Aires. I saw her once again; she could only talk about conspiracies, persecutions, and cataclysms; quite paranoid; I lost track of her after that.

Paso de las Nubes was a beautiful traverse along the bottom of the Cerro Tronador all the way to Chile. Again with Ferruccio and Mario, but this time with Mario's sister Sandra. We cut the bamboo-like reeds to make pallets on which we laid the sleeping bags to sleep on the rocks next to the roaring creeks. Fast-forward: Mario, after that summer, kept sending me pictures of our trek together, with warm messages written on the back; then one day he sent me a telegram: "Do not delay in coming; I am waiting for you." Then there was an express letter talking about God and good and evil. My father said "He is mad." Next, I got a request from his family to send back all the correspondence from him; it was needed for proper treatment because he indeed had had a psychotic breakdown and was in the hospital. Mario did recuperate; I saw him again in Bariloche, at the Balseiro Institute when GF gave a course there in 1970. The incident from 15 years earlier was not brought up; Mario was married and seemed well.

The Lagunitas was another memorable hike. I went there with the weekly excursion of the CAB and found that the hikers were a group of slovenians — Anička, Arko, Ivan — with whom I became fast friends. On this excursion the first night was spent under a huge hanging rock, known as La Piedrita. We each took a plank of wood on the way up for the hut that the slovenians were building, encasing the space under the rock. The next day we hiked up to the two lakes, or Lagunitas; there was a party of notable old-timers there, for the lakes were being named Tonçek and Schmall, after the two slovenian mountain climbers who had just lost their lives the previous year, in an avalanche while climbing the Paine Grande in Chile. I had met Tonçek when he made a presentation to the CABA. The notable old-timers at the dedication of the lakes included Emilio Frey who must have been 80 years old and was still climbing up mountains. Frey played numerous important roles in the area since the beginning of the 1900s: he was part of the negotiating team that dealt with the border conflicts that raged between Argentina and Chile; he became head of the area's national parks; he was a founder of the CAB in 1931. Fast forwarding: in 1957 a hut was built next to the Lagunitas and named Refugio Frey. I stayed there with a friend in 1970 when GF was giving a course at the Instituto Balseiro. Most people now arrive at the Refugio Frey via the ridge of the Cerro Catedral — where we had camped that winter when the boys tried to climb the Needles. But we took the old route (now known as the Picada Eslovena) that goes by the Piedrita (now known as the Refugio Esloveno), where the amancay (known as peruvian lilies in the USA) cover the slopes.

Some of the slovenians in Bariloche had been partisans fighting the Germans during WWII, fleeing communism after the war. When they settled in Argentina they chose a landscape that was similar to that of their native land, with lakes and mountains. Ivan had a photography shop named Triglav and I had assumed that it was his family name, Ivan Triglav. Many years later, when GF gave a course at the Physics Institute in Trieste, we took a trip to Yugoslavia and started off in Slovenia, motivated by my fond remembrances of my slovenian friends. I was surprised and amused to find that Triglav was not Ivan's name (as I afterwards corroborated) but the name of the most important mountain peak in Slovenia.

The end of the summer school was memorable because we came back to Buenos Aires in an army DC3 (with bench seats running the length the plane along the sides): it was my first airplane flight ever.

Patagonia 50 years later

At the turn of the century, 1999 and 2000, Paoli (our daughter, then in her early 30s) and I (in my late 60s) flew the very new airplane route from Buenos Aires straight to El Calafate (in the province of Santa Cruz). We had been there before, to celebrate my 60th birthday as a family. At that time the planes only flew into Rio Gallegos, on the coast, and one took a bus for the long 320-kilometer ride over the flat plateau to Calafate. Calafate is smack on the Andes, next to fabulous glaciers, among them the Perito Moreno that has become a big tourist attraction. In recent years Calafate has been much talked about because it is the home of two recent presidents, Nestor and Cristina Kirchner. For the mountain trekker and climber, it is the gateway to the Fitz Roy massif, made famous by Yvon Chouinard on the logo of his Patagonia-brand gear. And that is where Paoli and I were headed, to El Chalten and a week of backpacking. This area, so far south, had been beyond reach of the common folk during my growing-up years, when Bariloche (northern Patagonia) was the center of our mountaineering activities. I was eager to explore it.

The first ascent of the Fitz Roy had been made, famously, by a french expedition in 1951. Several members of CABA had a close relationship with members of the french expedition. I have here the account, in its spanish version, of the 'Assault of the Fitz Roy' written by L. Depasse and dedicated 'bien sympathiquement' to me. Depasse lived in Argentina and was ski instructor for the CABA group when we stayed in the army barracks in 1953. He had been a ski instructor in Chamonix in his youth and this connection with the french climbers resulted in his being a part of the 'assault' expedition. The ties with CABA members led to a visit by the french climbers to the factory in

Escobar (which they compared to their own training grounds outside Paris on the boulders of Fontainebleau) and in an asado (barbeque) that I missed because at the time I was in France. However I did attend an asado two years later when the french returned to climb the south face of the Aconcagua, an expedition where all but one of them had to have toes or fingers amputated because of frostbite.

The backpack with Paoli took us through magnificent terrain and gorgeous vistas. We had our share of adventures, such as the crossing of a raging fast-flowing river which to me was terrifying because I knew that Poinceneau, a member of the french expedition in 1951, had drowned in fast-flowing shallow water in the approach to the Fitz Roy. Paoli, strong and experienced outdoors woman that she is, crossed the river several times to take my backpack and to offer me stability with her pole, so I did get across … before dark. The problem was that I had been using an old map — stupid thing to do — that showed there was a bridge there; we could, in fact, see its remains; but we missed seeing the new trail that obviated that crossing.

This incident is one of several during backpacks with Paoli when she came to the rescue. Another that comes to mind was in Bariloche in 1984. Paoli was 16 and already an experienced outdoors woman. I had wanted to share my Patagonian 'backyard' with her. During a traverse from Cerro Lopez to Cerro Negro I got stuck on the trail: to the left a wall of rock; to the right a steep fall into a very cold lake; I was standing on a ledge and it was necessary to boulder up — climb using hands — perhaps 8 feet. I could not bring myself to go forward. Eventually I handed my backpack to Paoli, who was ahead of me, and clambered up uneventfully. It took a fair amount of coaxing by Paoli. She's a fabulous mountain guide.

At the end of our 2000 trip, Paoli and I decided we would return the next summer to the Andes on the other side of the border in Chile, behind the Fitz Roy. We would backpack the circuit around the Torres del Paine. That we did, and it was magnificent: varied terrain, and lakes, glaciers and the continental ice fields nearby. I described it in an article I had hoped to publish in a newspaper at a time (post-retirement) when

I thought I'd like to be a travel writer. The Paine trek article was well received at the Los Angeles Times but ultimately did not get published. My planned new career (I was ready to write about Colonia del Sacramento in Uruguay) never took off because I got involved in other projects.

The Musketeers. Aside from being an expert mountaineer and guide, my younger daughter Paoli is a yoga instructor and biomechanist, founder of Bozeman Center for the Healing Arts. In 2009 Paoli held a yoga retreat in Bariloche. Several of her students came from the USA for the week-long event, as did my three high school friends from Buenos Aires — the Musketeers. I am the youngest, so, as I write this, the three of them are 87; very active, curious, engaged. They take buses and the subway to mobilize themselves all over Buenos Aires to take in the cultural events, try out different eating places, visit new urban projects. Of course, I join them when I am there. And they joined me in Bariloche. Which made it a celebration because the three of us had been there together exactly 60 years earlier, in 1949; at that time we had just finished high school, and the whole class (about 25 of us) was celebrating with a trip to the lakes and mountains.

Patagonia 80 years later

As I reread my writings before sending this book to print, I find myself at the start of yet another Patagonia adventure. As befits my age, it's not a mountaineering adventure this time. But it seems a fitting finale to a love affair which started in the north, went on in the south, and now ends in the middle of Patagonia, an area that is opening up last.

I'm undertaking a project with the Tompkins Conservation Foundation and my colleague, Leandro Panetta. I just signed the contract, made my donation to the cause, and received via FedEx several magnificent coffee table books on other finished projects of the Tompkins Foundation. The project at hand is the development of a Visitor Complex in an area that is close to the UNESCO Heritage of the Humanity Site of Cueva de las Manos. The Visitor Complex will include an interpretation center of the local flora, fauna, geology, ethnography, and astronomy. The

Tompkins Foundation plans a Binational Patagonia Park with uninterrupted terrain from both sides of the Andes: Chile and Argentina. My personal involvement began with a mutual wish to work together with Leandro — who designed the existing interpretive center on the Chile side of Patagonia Park — and to contribute to the great work done by the Tompkins Conservation Foundation (that acquires land, creates infrastructure, and then donates the land back to the federal governments of the countries involved for conservation and public use). What drew me to the area is the existence of an observatory, a very primitive structure built to shield observers of the skies from the patagonian winds and chill. I have added a Pathway to the Sky to the project, which includes a trail with lookouts that suggest to visitors interactive activities relating to the sun and to the moon. It also includes a planetarium that can contrast southern and northern skies at the same latitude, as well as

My Patagonia:

(1) is my Patagonia of the 1940s and '50s;

(2) is my Patagonia of the 1980s and '90s;

(3) is my Patagonia of 2020.

show the polar skies in both hemispheres (explaining how they change over millennia — millennia gone by since the original inhabitants of the Cueva de las Manos, and millennia to come). These ideas came from a Polar Project proposal I had written up in the 1990s for an exhibition that never came to pass.

It is so satisfying that this notion of giving value to our southern sky will hopefully finally come to fruition. It is now happening, and the timeline calls for opening in December 2022 — a celebration of my 90th birthday!

2007 Trekking south of the 42nd parallel
Notes and stories compiled for the Big 75 Viaje trippers[1]

If you look at the world head-on as if you were an astronaut flying over the South Pole, you will see a large land mass (Antarctica) surrounded by a vast ocean. Out of that ocean, two narrow tongues of land jut out, straining towards the Pole. They are South America and New Zealand, the world's most southerly regions inhabited by humans, springboards to Antarctica. Polar explorers, scientific researchers and, more recently, tourists, all take off from one of three places: Ushuaia in Argentina, Punta Arenas in Chile, or Christchurch in New Zealand.

We don't usually think of New Zealand and South America as being next-door neighbors. Yet if you set off, say, from Christchurch and travel along parallel 42 in either direction, you will not come upon any land until you reach South America (Chile if you set out to the East; Argentina if you set out to the West); there is nothing but water in between.

There is something special about being on the border of the hinterland, the edge of civilization. The sudden gusts of cold wind blowing in from the South remind you constantly that you are near the Antarctic ice. Yet, on the 42nd parallel there is a green, white and blue beauty: the forests, the glaciers and the lakes. There is also silver and grey: grey rocks from the moraines, silver-grey tree trunks of driftwood.

For my daughter Paola, to arrive in New Zealand from a (Southern) summer of research work in Antarctica was to step into a paradise of color. "The unrelenting whiteness of the ice-cap gets to you after a

---

1 In 2007 I celebrated my 75th birthday in Argentina with a day (including an *asado*) in an *estancia* (a ranch). The 100 guests included 20 friends from the USA, hikers all, and for them I compiled this write-up.

while," she said. What also got to her was the sense of living in a prison cell with invisible walls. For in spite of the vastness of the Antarctic continent, her movements were restricted by regulations designed to safeguard the fragile ecology, and it wasn't possible to simply take off and explore. New Zealand offered relief, providing boundless freedom to wander about.

In 1998, hiking with Janet S. in New Zealand's South island, I thought: "Is this what Patagonia would be like if the British had colonized it?" It seemed so orderly, so neat, so civilized. So easy. Things are never that easy in South America…

1999: A Trek in Chile's Southern Patagonia

The narrow tip of South America that reaches out to Antarctica, with Chile on one side of the Andes and Argentina on the other, is known locally as el Cono Sur (the Southern Cone). The southernmost portion of the Cono Sur is Patagonia, a geographical area loosely defined without reference to political boundaries. Seventeen hundred miles south of the capital cities of Santiago and Buenos Aires is southern Patagonia, a remote region of remarkable rugged beauty and harsh climate. There you find the largest icefields on earth as well as lakes, glaciers and icebergs, forests, rocky mountains, and the relentless patagonian wind that often blows in gale-force gusts. That is where we've gone trekking, my daughter and I, in Torres del Paine National Park. Our aim is to do the six-day walk around the Paine massif, a dramatic outcropping of granite that juts 7,000 feet out of the surrounding plains.

As a young woman in Argentina, where I was born, I'd go skiing and backpacking in Patagonia. But that was in the northern reaches, for in those days, the early 1950s, the extreme South was quite inaccessible and unexplored. As time went by and the area opened up to travelers, I dreamed of extending my youthful expeditions further south. When my daughter Paola said she wanted to come with me, it all fell into place. Paola is a strong outdoors woman who has opted out of Southern California to live in Montana, with the Rockies as her backyard. She is fluent in Spanish, which made it possible to hire a local guide and go native.

Through the Internet I found Edmundo, our guide. His name, very appropriately, rhymes with "fin del mundo" — world's end — which pretty much describes southern Patagonia. Edmundo is part owner of Andescape, a firm that owns many of the mountain shelters in Paine Park. He e-mailed that, certainly, they would take care of shelter, food and transportation. We just needed our backpacks with our personal gear and sleeping bags. So in December, mid-summer in the Southern Hemisphere, we happily took off.

To get to Torres del Paine National Park we flew to Santiago and changed planes to Punta Arenas, the southernmost city in Chile and closest airport to the Park. This distance is just about the same as from Los Angeles to southern Alaska. We did it all in one fell swoop, arriving in Punta Arenas at noon, 17 hours after leaving California. As we were about to land, the pilot announced that the temperature was 48° Fahrenheit. Hardly the balmy weather I'd imagined when I packed a swimsuit for taking refreshing breaks in running brooks. But we were, after all, in Charles Darwin country. Darwin, who had been in the vicinity navigating through the Beagle Canal in January 1832, wrote in his *Journal*: "The summer solstice was now passed, yet every day snow fell on the hills... The thermometer generally stood about forty-five degrees, but in the night fell to thirty-eight or forty..." When we got off the plane the wind was howling, as it would every day of our stay.

Punta Arenas is built on the northern shore of the Strait of Magellan, a 40-miles-wide stretch of water that connects the Atlantic and the Pacific Oceans. The city of Punta Arenas saw great glory at the end of last century, when ships going West from Europe to the Pacific had to go through the Strait of Magellan. The boom ended abruptly with the opening of the Panama Canal in the early 1900s. But what a town it must have been during the golden years! Settlers from Europe developed the first sheep ranches and, as they prospered, built themselves luxurious homes. They brought artisans from Italy and Germany and Spain to paint frescoes, carve wooden mantlepieces, build furniture. Some of these small palaces are still standing and worth visiting.

We weren't meeting Edmundo until the next day, so we took ourselves to our hotel, the Cabo de Hornos. Cabo de Hornos, meaning

Cape of the Ovens, is an incorrect rendering in Spanish of Cape Horn, which was named for the birth-town of one of its Dutch discoverers. Cape Horn is the southernmost tip of the Southern Cone, the last bit of land facing Antarctica. It lies 200 miles south of Punta Arenas.

Three hours north of Punta Arenas by car or bus is the town of Puerto Natales, our point of departure for Torres del Paine; the Park is yet another three hours drive. An alternate route to Puerto Natales is by ferry boat from Puerto Montt in the Lake District. This is a popular but somewhat uncertain trip, due to vagaries in weather and schedules. It takes three days, sailing along scenic fjords and islands.

Puerto Natales cannot be reached directly by land from northern Chile, for someplace around 44° latitude south the country breaks up into an archipelago that can only be negotiated by boat. The connection by land between the extreme south of Chile and the rest of the country is via Argentina. This is the way locals commute to Santiago. The route over the Andes to Argentina — six hours of not-so-good road — is also used by tourists who want to take in the National Parks in both countries. The result of this geography is that, as a Chilean who handled pack horses put it, "We feel closer to our Argentinian neighbors than to our fellow Chileans up north." In fact, he was dressed exactly like an Argentinian gaucho from the pampas, in soft black boots and spurs, the wide trousers *(bombachas)*, six-inch-wide leather belt with silver ornaments, long-sleeved shirt and vest, and a colorful *boina* (a Spanish-style cap).

En route to the Torres del Paine, not far from Puerto Natales, the road goes by a cave where the remains of a milodón were found. The milodón is a giant prehistoric sloth that is thought to have lived from five to ten thousand years ago, co-existing with humans. The first scientists that dealt with this discovery were Europeans, who took the remains back home with them. Nowadays this kind of expatriation is no longer possible, for the Instituto de Estudios Patagónicos, founded in 1969, has taken over control of paleontological sites. Originally this milodón was named after Florentino Ameghino, the father of South American paleontology. But now it is called milodón *darwinii*, for although Darwin never set foot precisely in this region, he had unearthed the first milodón in the Argentinian Patagonia during his famous voyage in 1832.

The Paine Park was established in 1959 but it is only over the past ten years that it has become an increasingly popular tourist destination. Undoubtedly this is due to the development of an infrastructure that makes this remote park remarkably user friendly. There are buses from Puerto Natales, camping facilities, and a fine system of wood huts modeled on the European alpine shelters. The huts *(refugios)* have bunks with mattresses and they are staffed, so one can buy ready-made meals. In the southern area of the massif the refugios are well-spaced, so it is possible to do a comfortable hut-to-hut trek.

We chose a more adventuresome route that called for longer hiking days and some tent-camping. This Big Circuit starts in the plain in full view of the Paine Towers *(Torres)*, climbs 3,600 ft to the Paine Pass (also called Garner Pass) from where the patagonian icefields come suddenly and dramatically into view, then descends to the icefields, glaciers and lakes on the plain below the Paine Horns *(Cuernos)*.

With daughter Paola in
Puerto Natales

A 3,600-foot pass may not sound very high or dramatic. Yet this pass was very similar to a Himalayan one I trekked in Nepal at 15,000 ft. The reason is that the Andes get lower the further south one goes, and at the Paine Pass, at 52° latitude south, snow and ice and the harsh climate are a result of being near the Pole. So one gets the magnificent sights and terrain typical of high mountains without having to battle the lack of oxygen.

When we began our trek north there were four of us in the party: Paola and I, Edmundo and his assistant-in-training Janeric. Later on, a young Spaniard, Javier, who worked at one of the Andescape huts, joined us too. Over the next few days we saw very few people, but plenty of wildlife. To a Californian hiker, used to being on the lookout for snakes and bears, Patagonia is a paradise where these creatures don't exist. There are pumas (mountain lions), but locals say they are rarely seen.

In the plains to the east of the mountains a small silver fox sat on the road, close to us. Patagonian hares, looking like big rabbits with huge ears, often ran in front of us, in and out of the bushes. In the lakes, white swans with black necks, pink flamingoes; nearby, upland geese ("They mate for life": everyone seemed impressed by this and wanted us to know). We also saw groups of guanacos, where the just-born little ones were nursing. Guanacos are wild relatives of the domes-ticated llamas found further north. The Indians hunted them for their meat and pelts. At one time it seemed that guanacos were in danger of extinction. Today, the guanacos subsist, but the Indians have all perished…

At first we walked in fields white with wild daisies. There were fast-flowing glacial streams: some we crossed on hanging bridges; others we forded with care. Edmundo insisted I hold on to his belt, for stories abound of people drowning in mountain streams that reach only to their calves. As we climbed, the vegetation and the terrain kept changing. Thorny *calafate* bushes, then short *ñires* and tall *lengas,* both of them beeches of the Nothofagus genus. All the trees in the forests of southern Patagonia are varieties of Nothofagus, which are found only in the south of the southern hemisphere, notably also in the New Zealand Fjordlands.

We spent the night in the Refugio Dickson, after crossing a river in a rubber boat that was powered by pulling, hand over hand, on a rope strung overhead from shore to shore. We had dinner with two Britishers who had just come over the pass, traveling in the opposite

Torres del Paine with guanacos

Trekking among the daisies

Elsa crossing a suspension bridge

direction from us. (By and large there were very few North Americans in the Park, but many Europeans). Much of the conversation was about weather conditions and how the pass had not been passable for several days due to poor visibility and snowfall. The two men told of sinking in the mud in swamps, and of having trouble finding the markers in the rocks because they were caught in a blizzard.

Pulling across the river to Refugio Dickson

The next day it was our turn to traverse bogs. The trick is to step on the tufts of grass that will hold your weight, for if you fall in you are weighted down by your backpack, and it is hard to find solid support to lift yourself out from the mud. After the bogs we came upon hanging glaciers and icebergs in mountain lakes. When we arrived at the campground up high, close to the pass, the caretaker offered us *mate* (pronounced *mah-teh*). Mate is an infusion, like tea, that is drunk out of a gourd, through a metal straw. It is the standard popular drink in the Cono Sur and is definitely an acquired taste. "Amargo?" he asks. Amargo means bitter, without sugar, the way the purists drink it. "Amargo!" we respond. A long mate-drinking session ensues, the gourd filled with hot water and passed from hand to hand in rigorous sequence.

I think this is when I realized that this trip was a double adventure, physical for me, cultural for Paola. She had found it annoying when the Chileans ribbed her without mercy for having 'gringo' habits such as not wanting to share her water bottle, or carrying a water filter and pump. By the time she accepted the mate amargo, however, she was a gringa no more.

With Paola,
Glaciar Los Perros

The day we crossed the Paine Pass the weather was glorious. A condor or two flew overhead. Hawks were looking for prey. It was December 21, summer solstice, with 18 hours of daylight. And a good thing this was, too, for the descent to the icefields, although exhilarating, was muddy, slippery, steep and studded with large fallen logs. It took us 13 hours to complete the day's hike. The sudden wind gusts, thankfully, come from the west so they push hikers into the side of the mountain rather than into the void. That night, almost at sea-level once more, at Refugio Grey, we had a wonderful meal of *chivito asado* (barbecued goat). Paola went out to do a bit of rock climbing by the light of the full moon. She enthused later: "It was so strange: Orion was upside down, and it moves from right to left. And I saw the Southern Cross quite high in the sky."

There is a legend that whosoever eats the calafate berry will always come back to Patagonia. Paola and I have already made plans to return but, just in case, not wanting to tempt fate, we stuff the calafate berries — sour and unripe as they are in December — into our mouths.

Musical Buenos Aires

A few months ago, a concert of the La Jolla Symphony featured a piece by a young musician who, in the program notes, talked about the strong influence on her career of Maestro Efrain Guigui. Goodness, I thought, I didn't know Guigui had become so prominent. This threw me right back to my adolescence in Buenos Aires, a time when Guigui the clarinetist, with Gerardo Levy, flutist, and Hermann Ehrenhaus, oboist, were the ubiquitous woodwinds in several symphonic orchestras. They played under the great directors of the time who visited Buenos Aires; one of them was Aaron Copeland, who — I found out when I googled Guigui and Levy — invited them to Tanglewood (a famed music school and summer festival in Massachusetts). They accepted and went in 1954, after which both of them stayed in the USA and had distinguished careers teaching, playing, and conducting.

Buenos Aires in the late 1940s and early 1950s was a hotbed of musical activities. These were the post–World War II years, when more than one hundred musicians who were forced to flee Europe during the Nazi years found refuge in Argentina. Most of them came to the country with excellent musical backgrounds, having studied in the best musical schools and with first-rate teachers; some had achieved successful professional lives in Europe. In their new country some set themselves up with studios — my piano teacher and my brother's violin teacher were in this category — others played in orchestras and chamber music groups. A small subgroup formed an institute, the Collegium Musicum, which became very influential and affected many lives, mine among them.

The Collegium Musicum

The idea for establishing a Collegium Musicum in Buenos Aires came from Wilhelm (Guillermo) Graetzer, who was inspired by music schools from his childhood days in Vienna. Like those schools, the Collegium would offer high-quality music instruction to children, amateurs, and teachers. Graetzer asked Erwin Leuchter and Ernesto Epstein, also trained in Vienna and Germany, to join him, and in 1946 the Collegium was founded. Later on Ljerko Spiller, violinist, and Teodoro Fuchs, conductor, also joined. The school created by these five extraordinary musicians has functioned uninterrupted to this day, offering everything from seminars on music in the middle ages, through classes on harmony, to choir-singing, recorder lessons, and Carl Orff method classes for children.

The Collegium marked the lives of my generation. My brother Hector sang in the choir, which gave yearly concerts and on occasion had extraordinary directors, like Klemperer (or was it Prohaska?) under whose baton they sang in the Teatro Colón. Hector and I studied harmony with Leuchter; we analyzed works by Bach and Mozart, and labored over the homework. I participated in seminars with Epstein (such as one on the music of Josquin des Prés and Guillaume de Machault), and attended lectures by Fuchs on orchestration and musical form.

Some of our fellow students with whom we were friendly moved to Europe in the 1950s and led notable lives: Miguel Gielen, Mauro Kagel, and Carlos Kleiber (the son of Erich Kleiber). Gielen was billed 'german conductor Michael Gielen' although his formative years were spent in Argentina; he conducted the foremost orchestras in Europe and the USA, and championed contemporary works. Kagel was born in Argentina of immigrant parents. He left to study electronic music in Köln (Cologne) and remained living in Europe, teaching, conducting, and composing. His activities spilled over into film and theater. His compositions are innovative and often border on the absurd. This is what my friends, who attended his concerts when he travelled back to Buenos Aires, told me. He is widely considered to be part of the avant-garde of musicians. Carlos Kleiber, who had been 'Karl' in his native Germany but kept his argentinian equivalent 'Carlos' all his life, conducted mostly in Germany but also in Britain and the USA. He was known for his attention to detail and discipline 'tempered with expressive vitality.' He retired from concert life at age 60 and became a recluse. Many consider him to be among the greatest conductors of all times.

Two of our talented women friends from the Collegium, Paola Loew and Iris Gonzala, also left for Europe in the 1950s, and married front-line concert pianists. Paola was my age and we were quite close. She and her family were italian. Early on I was surprised that at age 16 or so, she smoked in public and her parents would even offer her cigarettes when they lit their own. I remembered the Vittorio De Sica movies with young urchins smoking in the streets of Rome. Paola said she had smoked from age 14: it was standard in post-war Italy. She was beautiful and sophisticated, studying to be a pianist. There was something very earthy and matter-of-fact about the family's take on life that I found intriguing — and somewhat frightening, I think: *September 1950. It's curious to note the different attitudes of people towards life. Yesterday Paola was telling me that at the end of next year she'd like to be ready to go to the USA and present herself to Horowitz to see if he'll take her on as a student. Then her family would leave Argentina because her parents had come only to give their children a good solid education which was not possible in Europe because of the war. Next year Paola would be 17 years old, a good age to start facing life by herself, and her parents — mission accomplished — could return to Italy. So Paola would be free to succeed or never make it beyond being a piano teacher. The parents would wash their hands: they gave her a good education and the means to face life; it is for Paola to manage by herself from now on.*

As it turned out: *April 1951. Paola was offered a contract to make movies and she accepted. She acted in two already and is starting on her third. "Of course, that will set her back in her piano career" I commented — I'm afraid I was trying to excuse my envy. XX answered "In her case I would have done the same. The years of piano she can recuperate later; but this way she lives a nice experience." I ruminated on her words and soon, very soon, I was convinced. I am beginning to understand the value of experience. Not all knowledge comes from books, Elsa!*

In the end, Paola did make acting her career, in the theater in Vienna and in films. But in Buenos Aires she was still juggling movies with her musical career. She was friends with the various young pianists who came to Buenos Aires to perform, in particular Sigi Weissenberg and Friedrich Gulda. *August 1952. Last week I was at Paola's. It was a get-together with the purpose of introducing her future husband, F. Gulda. He played for us doing some fabulous imitations of other pianists; also, he produced extraordinary variations in the style of Bach, Mozart, Falla, Hindemith. We laughed a lot.* Paola was married to Gulda for ten years. They had two sons; she sent me an announcement when the first one was born; he was named Wolfgang after Mozart.

Our other Collegium woman friend, Iris Gonzala, sang in the choir with my brother; she had a wonderful voice and was extremely musical; but singing remained a hobby and she became a ceramicist in Vienna, producing pottery busts that were very inventive caricatures of well-known people. Iris married Alfred Brendel. They were married for twelve years and had a daughter, Doris, who is a successful pop rock musician. When Doris was little, the three of them came to visit me and we spent the whole afternoon, at their request, at the San Diego Zoo (which is, indeed, well-known and very worthwhile).

The Camping Musical Bariloche

During the summer of 1955 that I spent at the Physics School in Bariloche, the very first weekend I went with a friend to visit the Camping Musical Bariloche, which was close by. We had been asked by friends in Buenos Aires to bring greetings for Ernesto Epstein (one of the cofounders of the Collegium Musicum), who was there in residence, teaching and writing. It was the first of several visits we made that summer to the Camping Musical, where there were always people we knew from the musical circles in Buenos Aires.

The Camping Musical Bariloche had been created five years earlier. Two of the handful of founders were Gerardo Levy and Efrain Guigui, the flutist and clarinetist I've already introduced. The Camping Musical started with professional musicians vacationing in a remarkably beautiful location on a lake, paying their way by giving concerts at the Bariloche library. Soon it evolved into an important summer school for young musicians, which draws students from all over the country and abroad.

The Teatro Colón

An opera house in the grand european tradition, the Colón Theater offers symphonic music, dance, and opera. It is acoustically superb (Pavarotti apparently called it 'perfect'). The building itself is majestic: built in 1806, its imposing entry halls and stairs boast italian marbles of different colors and gold-plated walls; the seats are scarlet velvet; in the ceiling, the central chandelier is surrounded by paintings by Soldi, one of Argentina's foremost artists. It is and was always magical to attend a performance there.

Because the season (winter) in Buenos Aires coincides with the off-season in Europe and the USA, it was possible to have the best artists at the Colón. When I was little my grandmother took me to see the Sakharoffs dancing: I vividly remember 'L'après midi d'un faune.' Among the great conductors I remember the sober elegance of Furtwangler and of Sargent. Among the virtuosi, Giesking and Arrau.

I went often to the Colón: with my mother, when I was young, we saw the classic ballets; with friends, during my teens, we went to hear everything symphonic. In my early twenties, HRR introduced me to opera — Mozart and Alban Berg, forget the in-betweens! (My broader opera education happened later, in the USA.) At the Colón, opera-lovers had the choice of three different subscriptions: one to german opera, another to french opera, and the third to italian opera. Although I never heard them at the Colón, I know that the greatest singers of the 20th century sang there — just as the greatest conductors, instrumentalists, and dancers of the 20th century performed there too.

Last year, the TEDX Rio de la Plata talks were held at the Teatro Colón in Buenos Aires. I was invited to participate in this event. You can imagine my emotions: for the first time not a spectator, but a performer on that hallowed stage.

Other venues, other people

In addition to the musical activity going on at the Colón, there were several musical societies that held their seasonal concerts elsewhere: the Wagneriana, the Mozarteum, and the 'Amigos de la Música' (Friends of Music, to which my parents had a subscription). To these (and other) concerts we (my friends and I) would sometimes go without tickets. We entered through the artists' entrance (easy to do, since we knew several of the members of the orchestra), and then grabbed empty seats if there were any or, if there weren't, sat in the orchestra pit. Oftentimes these escapades became a game of musical chairs: if we sat down and then the actual ticket-holders appeared, we would apologize for our 'mistake' and move to another set of empty seats; and so on…

There were also Sunday morning concerts where I heard Gulda, and Sigi Weissenberg, and Byron Janis, and Badura-Skoda playing duets with Jorg Demus. All these pianists were very young, just a few years older than me. So the hall was full of fans, young girls who would jump on the stage to request autographs. Fast forwarding: last year (2018), Badura-Skoda and Demus, both ninety years old, still playing together, gave a duet concert in Vienna.

One of our friends who played violin in an orchestra and in a chamber music group was Leo Spierer. He was part of our small group that got together at the house of Paola Loew on weekends; we played a highly intellectual version of 'charades' and sometimes played music. *September 1952. Last night we went to Paola's. She and Leo played together what they are playing today in a benefit concert. I turned the pages. The remaining five listened. It was really nice. Then we had dinner, put on jazz records and Leo and Paoli danced. They were funny and made us laugh.*

Leo also left for Europe. He settled in Berlin and became concertino (first violin) of the Berlin Philharmonic, playing under Herbert von Karajan.

Another friend, Vera Graf, also played the violin. She came to the USA to study, and was in New York when I was there too. Vera was hired to play in the orchestra at Tanglewood. There she met Erich Leinsdorf and they got married. I saw them several times on the west coast, when Leinsdorf conducted in San Diego and in Los Angeles. GF got along very well with Leinsdorf: they had the same viennese sense of humor. The first time they came to San Diego I wasn't here, I was in Argentina. But GF knew Vera was my friend and he invited them for bagels and lox. Over coffee, Leinsdorf asked GF what he did for a living. GF said "I work in physics of the solid state; you know, transistors and semiconductors…" And Leinsdorf replied: "Semiconductors, ah, yes, I've known several those…"

Finally, I want to talk about Jorge Milchberg, who became a good friend after we overlapped while backpacking in the mountains south of Bariloche. He also went to Europe in the 1950s and settled in Paris. Jorge made his name with folk music. He founded a group he called Urubamba, after the river in Peru. The group played music of the people of the Andes with the original instruments, quenas and charangos. When I saw the group in concert, there were four people sitting on the floor of the stage in a circle with a heap of instruments in the middle. As they played, they picked their instruments from the heap, as needed. One of the tunes they played was 'El cóndor pasa', which was later popularized by Paul Simon. Simon and Milchberg became friends and in the 1970s did some recording together.

The concert I attended with my daughters was in 1982 in Buenos Aires. Jorge and I had not seen each other for thirty years. When we went backstage to greet him after the concert he asked: "Do you still have the white piano?" A sure sign that he knew exactly who I was. It turned out that we left Buenos Aires on the same day and both of us had to change planes in Galeão, the airport of Rio de Janeiro; so we chatted again and, in Galeão, I wrote a ditty that I later sent him. It has the rhythm of a tango and some slang:

Oda a Jorge Milchberg:
Te acordás hermano qué tiempos aquellos
En que a Bariloche íbamos a escalar,
Y de grampones y picos munidos
Por los glaciares quisimos pasar?

En una cabaña con pastor de ovejas,
Con las Girl Scout galas te fuiste a encontrar,
Y en un camión repleto de cosas
Del Bolsón viajamos en noche estival.

Te accordás hermano qué tiempo sin mangos
En que a los conciertos s'iba uno a colar;
Antes de Urubamba y de los charangos,
Cuando el piano blanco solías tocar?

Por el mundo ahora estamos esparcidos,
Yo en California y vos en Paris,
Pero se cruzaron nuestros dos caminos
En BAires y Rio, '82 feliz.

No dejes hermano que el tiempo nos pierda,
Que otros treinta años pasen sin volver
A vernos las caras y estrechar las manos:
Amigos de otrora dan sentido al ser.

The early years

The 1950s were magical for me. The Collegium sucked me into a whirl-wind of musical experiences shared with extraordinary people. Music became — and remains — an essential part of my life. I don't think this would have been the case otherwise, since my family (myself included) was only moderately musical.

The piano. Mother played the piano quite well, and there was a lovely guitar hanging in the closet under the stairs that she had strummed in the boat trip to Europe during her honeymoon. The piano was a magnificent half-size ('media cola') Erard, bought in Paris during my parents' honeymoon in 1925. It had been painted in off-white enamel as was the fashion at the time. Still white, still magnificent to play almost 100 years later, the piano is in my apartment in Buenos Aires. My mother played Falla 'El amor brujo,' Granados, Albeniz ... and she practiced my piano lessons at night so that — as she said — I would know my lesson well that week. This is the piano Milchberg remembered; it was played every time we had our musical friends over.

I started music lessons at age 8, as was proper for children of the educated bourgeoisie. I had the same teacher for 10 years, a wonderful Czech emigré who was strict but kind (unlike the other leading piano teacher in the city at the time, Scaramuzza, who was strict but unkind). My teacher was Eugenio (Evgen) Bures (with the accent on the e in Spanish, but on the u in Central European languages). His wife, Hedi, had been a singer in Europe, but she never made a career for herself in Buenos Aires. In fact, thinking back, she probably never really made a life for herself in the New World: she was shy and liked to talk to me about my studies as I became older and started studying at the university; we would sit and talk on the steps of the stairs in their house while her husband finished with the lesson prior to mine. They had no children; just two greyhound dogs. Weekends they went to the islands in the Tigre Delta. They seemed to have no social life at all. When once my mother invited them for dinner, Hedi seemed ill at ease. She wore hats in the shape of turbans. Her dress seemed very antiquated to me. It was probably high style in the Europe she had left behind. Many years later, some friends of GF, the Hornaks, escaped communist Czechoslovakia, and we sponsored them to come to the USA. The wife, Vera, dressed in central european elegance, seemed totally out of place in southern California, just like Hedi Bures had seemed in Buenos Aires. Many years later I found out that Hedi was the talented daughter of a very well-known musician, Franz Schreker, whose blossoming career was destroyed by WWII. His work is now, in the XXIst century, being revived.

I said I was (am) only moderately musical; by this I mean I don't have a very good ear. Because I cannot play by ear, I read music quite well. In Buenos Aires I had reached a technical level where I was playing Chopin's Polonaises. I now stay with Mozart, Bach, and Scarlatti.

The violin. My brother, Hector, was assigned the violin. His first teacher was a bizarre hungarian lady who, apparently, taught him a technique that made playing impossible. After being straightened out by Napolitano — the concertino of the Teatro Colón — Hector went on to study for years with Mrs. Reyes, who was married to an american but who herself was hungarian and had been the student of Mischa Elman. So my brother's musical pedigree was quite impressive. Mrs. Reyes came to our house once a week, and tea and cakes were served in the dining room after the lesson. I was 6 years younger than my brother; nevertheless, I was allowed to listen in on the conversation about musical events and personalities. In later years, Hector took lessons with Ljerko Spiller, legendary master, who lived to be 100 lucid years old; I last saw him in his late nineties at my brother's second wedding.

Musical Buenos Aires

Playing our instruments and going to concerts gave us (my brother and me) a basic musical education. But it was the whirlwind of the musical Buenos Aires of the '50s that took us from a tame and adequate musical world to one that was overwhelmingly alive and brimming with excitement. *October 1952. Tuesday I went to the opening of Wozzeck. It was excellent. I liked it infinitely more than I thought I would.* In New York, Wozzeck didn't open until 5 years later. HRR and I, with the Argentinian arrogance and chauvinism we displayed when we first arrived in the USA, were dismayed by the musical backwardness of New York.

In truth we were privileged to have grown up in such a rich musical environment. I have been asked if it remains that way. Yes, it does. The legacy of those earlier years keeps Buenos Aires very musical indeed.

My professional life

If someone had asked me when I was 20 what I was going to do with a degree in physics, I could not have answered "I'll direct a team of developers of interactive exhibits at a science center" — because interactive science centers did not yet exist. In truth I didn't have the foggiest notion what I was going to do with my PhD, and it took me quite a while to 'find my passion' — as we tell young people to do. In fact, the fifteen years I spent developing exhibitry, and their aftermath, were the most satisfying of my professional life. Why, and what did it take to get there? The why can be stated briefly: because the work in the science center made use of all the capabilities and experience that I had amassed along the way in prior years. I felt particularly well suited for the job, found the work engaging, and was successful at it. What it took is the topic of the next section.

Collecting experience on the way to the Science Center[1]

Experimental physics. After passing the qualifying exams at Columbia University, a graduate student becomes a PhD candidate and starts looking for a faculty member who will sponsor the thesis work. Passing the qualifying exams at Columbia was no mean feat since they were designed as a filter to bring down the large number of entering students into a manageable group of doctoral students consistent with the number of faculty who could act as mentors. HRR and I, recently arrived from Buenos Aires with the equivalent of USA Master's degrees, unacquainted with the american mode of taking exams, failed miserably.

---

[1] This title purposefully mimics the one used by GF in his memoirs: 'Picking Flowers on the Way to Photosynthesis.'

March 14, 1958. Difficult times. Those frightful exams, that huge effort, that horrid oral, that big failure, that great weariness. We were not used to written exams which needed to be finished in a given amount of time that, in our estimation, was too short. We were given the opportunity to take the tests again, and a few months later we passed and were on our way.

Both of us wanted to do theoretical physics. I shot high: we had taken a course in statistical mechanics taught by T.D. Lee, who dazzled me with his brilliance. He was very gracious, gave me a paper to read, and when I went back to see him a few weeks later he asked me some questions I did not know what to do with, so he didn't take me on. The recommendation I got was that I should do experimental work.

I went to see Charles Townes who was working on masers and lasers, had a large group of students, and could use more. His laboratories on the 11th floor of Pupin Hall were known as the Radiation Lab because that is where work on microwave radiation and radar was done during World War II. When I joined his group in 1959, Townes had already produced the first maser (acronym for microwave amplification by stimulated emission of radiation) and developed the theory of the laser (substitute the word light for the word microwave in the acronym) and was intent on producing the first device. (He did not.) The first masers were gaseous devices, big and unwieldy. The search was on for solid state materials (crystals) that had the right properties and could be used instead. The problem that Townes gave me was to grow certain crystals that he thought would have the right properties (spin-relaxation times), and test them. I did not succeed in growing the crystals. Then along came GF, who was working on solid state masers at neighboring Bell Telephone Labs. (He was a visiting professor that year at Columbia University.)

GF, a consummate crystal-grower (for radios) from his days in Israel, saw that I was getting nowhere. So GF produced another problem using ready-made crystals (of magnesium oxide, MgO, with paramagnetic impurities), slightly deforming them by squeezing (along a crystal axis, using a special rig), and assessing how the properties (the spectroscopic lines of electron spin resonance of the impurities) change (this was my thesis result: they move and broaden). These experiments were carried out at low temperatures (liquid helium) and microwave frequencies. GF had the equipment set up at Bell Labs so I did the preliminary experiments there, in New Jersey. GF became my de facto thesis advisor.

Before I move my story to California, a few more words about Columbia and Townes. Aside from me, GF was also supposed to mentor my office-mate, Arno Penzias. Arno developed a maser that was used as an amplifier in a radio telescope. A few years after getting his PhD Arno went to work at Bell Telephone Labs, where he pursued his astronomical interest, using a radio telescope to look at the Milky Way. The telescope detected a signal, but Arno and his colleague Wilson could not explain its origin. They thought it was simply noise, a spurious signal; perhaps bird poop? Arno consulted with R.H. Dicke (a physicist at Princeton University), who had worked on the theory of cosmic micro-wave background radiation, and was looking for observational confir-mation of his theory. Dicke recognized Arno's 'noise' signal to be the cosmic radiation coming from the Big Bang that originated the universe. In 1978 Arno and Wilson received the Nobel Prize for this discovery. GF and I sent Arno congratulations, and a box of matzos to eat with the celebratory champagne, as a memento of the Columbia days when Arno munched matzos for lunch in our office. He recip-rocated, sending us t-shirts with the inscription: "This is the way the world began, not with a whimper but with a bang" (a takeoff on the line by T.S. Eliot "This is the way the world ends, not with a bang but a whimper").

In the summer of 1980, Arno threw a huge party to celebrate the 65th birthday of Charlie Townes. At this time Townes was at the University of California in Berkeley but he wanted to have the festiv-ities in San Diego so he could spend time at his favorite zoo. So Arno came out here and we decided to do the main event at our house. It was a wonderful celebration with people from all over the world.

Some more about Townes. His work on the maser earned him the Nobel Prize in 1964. At that time GF and I were in Argentina, working for a couple of months at the University of Buenos Aires, setting up a lab for paramagnetic resonance. We heard the announcement of Townes' prize when we were in Iguazú, so we sent him a postcard that shows how the water falls in several levels. It was an 'in' reference to his work on the maser, which relies on jumps of electrons between atomic energy levels.

When I came to California to join GF, in 1961, the first task was to set up the labs. Together with Roger Isaacson and Shelly Schultz, I helped set up the paramagnetic resonance lab, the one with the smaller permanent magnet. (There was also a nuclear magnetic resonance lab that had a huge permanent magnet.) One of my tasks was to make the modulation coils — enameled copper wire with a rectangular cross-section wound into flat pancake shapes — that were glued on to the poles of the magnet. Just around that time our papers were finally in order and GF and I got married — with Walter Kohn and my brother as witnesses. We wanted a civil ceremony and had a difficult time finding a justice of the peace. But GF located Judge Bone, who married us in Vista. When it was time for the usual exchange of rings I said, "We don't do rings." GF said, "Oh yes we do" and to my utter disbelief pulled out a box, opened it — and inside was a lovely ring made out of the modulation-coils wire. He then pulled out a larger box and said: "The enamel will eventually come off so I made you several replacements."

In 1964, we moved our transitory offices and labs from the Scripps Institution of Oceanography to the new campus of UCSD, now ready for occupancy. It was a spectacle to see the permanent magnets on a flat truck winding their way ever so slowly up the hill, from the beach to the mesa.

On the upper campus everything had to be set up from scratch. I got to design the layout of the small magnet lab including drawings for the carpentry shop to make consoles and tables; I loved doing this. When the machine shop was up and running, all the physics graduate students had to pass a test on the use of the metal cutter, the drill, the vertical saw and, most delicate of all, the milling machine; we were given a drawing with dimensions and had to mill a piece of brass accordingly. It looked like a dreidel. I was proud of my product and gave it as a present to my parents.

When the small magnet lab was operational I ran the last experiments for my thesis. I had found an excellent crystal that gave a beautiful spectrum, and I was going to record this trace (graph) for the publication of my work. The crystal, mounted in the resonant cavity, was a 1-inch by ½-inch by ¼-inch item that I left on a small ashtray on my desk for the next morning's experiment. But the next morning it was gone. Despair set in. Someone suggested the cleaning crew had thrown it out. It turned out they had, and it was in the trash truck that, thankfully, was still in the service yard. We collected several graduate students and began sifting through the trash, looking for such a small object that it really was a needle in a haystack. It's uncanny but we found it.

By 1964 I was done with my thesis; from Columbia University they sent me the final exam, which I duly took, and then I flew to New York to take the final orals and pass the thesis defense. When I came back to La Jolla we threw a garden party — 'Déjeuner sur l'herbe' we called it in the invitations — with skits and songs and Kentucky fried chicken in Baskin Robbins empty ice-cream containers. The physics department was still small so everybody was there — Walter Kohn, Maria and Joe Meyer, and also my parents, who were returning from an egyptology meeting in India.

For the next 5 years I held a research position at UCSD, did more experiments, and published a couple of articles beyond the thesis. (Out of sheer curiosity last year I joined a citation site, academia.edu, and I find, to my delight, that those articles are still being cited, occasionally). On paper I was part of the group of Bernd Mathias since nepotism rules barred me from doing paid work in GF's group. Bernd was a friend and poker buddy of GF's of long standing. He was, with GF, Walter Kohn, and Harry Suhl, one of the foursome that worked at Bell Labs who were recruited by Roger Revelle to start the physics department at UCSD (called UCLJ = UCLaJolla in those days).

Teaching and learning. 1965 was the first year there were undergraduate students at UCSD. I was recruited to be a section leader for one of the discussion groups of the large introductory physics class taught by Bob Swanson. At the end of this academic year, our first daughter, Shoshanah, was born. I was very moved when two girls in my discussion group gave me a present for my new baby. I had no family in San Diego nor anywhere in the USA, so the students' gesture was particularly meaningful.

This teaching assignment turned out to be important: I was very successful at it and enjoyed it a lot. I realized then that I much preferred interacting with students to being in the lab twirling knobs. In these days of career counseling, I might have learnt this much sooner; but it's not clear to me that it would have made that much difference in my career path. At the time, however, other situations came into play that resulted in a shift in direction: GF's sabbatical that we took in Boston and motherhood.

During the year in Boston I became intimately acquainted with several of the new curricula that were being developed in the wake of Russia's deployment of the first artificial satellite, Sputnik. The scare of losing the race for space to Russia prompted the US government to appropriate funds for the development of new programs to better train US youth in science. These new programs — variously called ESS, IPS, PSSC, HPP, BSSC, ESSC, SAPA, AAAS — were generically and infor-mally known as the 'alphabet soup.' The first four were being developed in Boston when we were there, spearheaded by scientists from Harvard and MIT. I worked for a while with the curriculum-development groups of ESS (Elementary Science Study, designed for primary schools), and IPS (Introductory Physical Science, designed for junior high school). At this time our second daughter, Paoli, had been born. I was deep into motherhood and fascinated with children's development. I began reading Piaget ('The Child's Conception of Physical Causality' and 'The Child's Conception of the World'), noticing the universal questions that children ask, such as: "Mummy, why does the moon always follow us when we move?" I found the ESS program extremely interesting; I went with program staff to the classrooms when they were testing their materials, and participated in the development of some of the units.

An important question that the ESS group grappled with was: "We have these beautiful materials; how do we get teachers to use them?"

One answer was 'summer workshops; provide in-service training to working teachers and let them train others in the school during the academic year.' For many years there were ample funds from the NSF (National Science Foundation) to carry out these training programs. But the truth was that, at the end of the summer workshops, the teachers went back to their previous teaching methods. So if people tend to teach the way that they were taught, the way to propagate the new materials was to teach them to prospective teachers while they were in college. I took this need to heart and came back to California with the purpose of doing just that: get a position at a teaching college and teach the ESS way.

In California at that time prospective teachers obtained a regular college degree that included one course in science; there was no college degree in education. In San Diego, the large teachers' college was San Diego State College which, eventually, became a university (SDSU). A remnant of the prior organization as a teachers' college was the department of physical science (later renamed natural sciences), which included faculty from heterogeneous fields of scientific expertise but with one goal in common: excellence in teaching and promotion of quality learning. One visit with the chair of this department and I got hired to develop the course I had in mind. I took a leave of absence from UCSD, but by 1969 I had a faculty position at SDSU and a full commitment to teaching there.

The ESS-based course that I developed grew over time into several semesters and we lobbied successfully (in Sacramento, the California state capital) to have one semester of it designated as required for teachers. It was so successful that over time it grew to three semesters; many students took the required semester and then one or two more as electives. What was special about this course? First of all, it was useful; years later former students told me they were still using their class notes to teach. The subject matter consisted mostly of ESS units that had been strung together to make up a meaningful college level course. Previously, students would choose classes on subject matter that was esoteric for children; black holes was a usual one in those days when they were all the rage in mainstream research. Second, the methodology of teaching was built in, so teachers were learning in the manner in which they would teach. Namely, the class observes a phenomenon, the teacher elicits explanations of how it occurs; the students then get to test their hypotheses; and class discussion of results follows. It's a hands-on process approach, the basic question being "How do we know what we know?"

After I had taught the course multiple times it became apparent that some concepts were consistently troublesome for some students. Also, specific misconceptions (or preconceptions or alternate conceptions — the name varied over time) and faulty reasoning appeared time and time again. Interesting, I thought, and contacted colleagues who were engaged in approaches to teaching similar to mine. Yes, they also were finding consistent 'errors in thinking.' How could one help the student supersede them? Shouldn't we describe our findings? Where could we publish them? To start out, a space was secured at the next American Physical Society meeting for a section with presentations on teaching and learning. The birth of this sub-specialty — research on teaching and learning done by scientists — can be dated to this meeting in 1979.

The new field had growing pains. It was extremely hard to get the attention — let alone the recognition — of the established scientists, those who think it's the student's fault if s/he doesn't understand a lecture. Therefore it was difficult for faculty members who did research on learning to get promoted. I was associate professor, had secured a grant from the National Science Foundation, had done and published research on learners' preconceptions, but had several uncomfortable setbacks before I was promoted to full professor.

During these teaching days I had students from a project in the education department who were going through their graduate work together, as a class. Half a dozen of them formed a closely knit group that took several seminars we developed on topics we were all interested in: free schools (Summerhill; this was the 70s, after all), Piaget. We went on trips together: the desert to do naked-eye astronomy, the mountains to hike and look at nature. Just the other day, after 40 plus years, I met one member of this group. "Remember when we wanted to do the ridge at 10,000 feet and it was too full of snow?" I asked. "Sure," he said, "we sat down and smoked pot and at the end we didn't know what to do with the roach and you <u>ate</u> it. And I thought, 'this woman is all right.'"

These years saw the birth of the discipline called cognitive science, a cooperative effort of several disciplines to understand understanding. I attended the founding meeting of this field at UCSD with Fred Reif, a good friend of GF's, a physicist from UC Berkeley, who shifted his research from hard science to teaching and learning. We had coincided in Boston and spent time at the MIT Media Lab together. Cognitive science is a powerful field that underpins much of the work being done at CRMSE, the Center for Research in Math and Science Education at SDSU. CRMSE was founded by Don Short, Dean of the School of Sciences, in collaboration with Sandy Marshall and myself. Several mathematicians at SDSU had been doing research in math learning, and three of us had been doing learning research in the sciences; it became clear that the time had come for creating a common site where we could interact. At CRMSE we also spearheaded a joint PhD program with interested faculty from UCSD. Graduate students came and got their doctorates. To this day, CRMSE is going strong.

Leadership. In 1980 I took the chair of the SDSU natural science department. The chairship is a 3-year elected position. I did not seek it. The prior chair made it happen: he thought I had leadership potential. And then I found out I was good at it, and developed a taste for it. I was good at calming irate professors when they came to complain about office or teaching assignments. I was good at managing meetings and moving them along. We hired two new faculty during my 3-year tenure, who became members of CRMSE.

The Science Center

And thus we come to 1983 and the job that uses all my accumulated expertise: experimental physics, teaching, research on learning, leadership. Science centers, or interactive science museums as we know them today, are an invention of the early 1980s. Arguably, the Chicago Museum of Science and Industry was a precursor, with its elliptical whisper room. But it was the Toronto Science Center (developed by Tuzo Wilson) and the Exploratorium in San Francisco that started the modern trend in the 1970s, and laid down a pedagogical philosophy. The Exploratorium was the brainchild of Frank Oppenheimer, a physicist who, like his brother Robert, had been laid off from the UC Berkeley faculty during the McCarthy era. Frank went to Colorado, where the family had a ranch, and took a high school teaching job. He had the idea that the laboratory should be a space that was open all the time, for the students to do experiments and explore on their own. This idea was the basis for the Exploratorium: a large space with stations where the visitor can carry out his/her own investigations.

My involvement with science centers began with a stay of several weeks at the Exploratorium, engineered by Jeff Kirsch, who was the newly appointed director of the Reuben H. Fleet Space Theater and Science Center, in San Diego's beautiful Balboa Park. Jeff Kirsch had been the producer of a TV segment for the local educational channel that featured my class in action during one of the summer NSF workshops for teachers, so he was familiar with my background. When he became director of the Reuben Fleet facility (which included the first huge-screen Omnimax theater in the USA), Jeff asked me what could be done with the big space that was the waiting area for the theater. I wrote a proposal for setting up a science center at the Reuben Fleet facility along the same lines as the Exploratorium. It was accepted and I started as a consultant to implement the project. As the job became more and more demanding and fascinating, I increased my time there and ended up with a full-time job. (The consultancy was treated as an educational grant to SDSU so I kept my faculty position.)

The idea was exciting. It was a novel way to extend to the general public what I had been doing until then, a task both novel and familiar. Many of the exhibits I had seen at the Exploratorium were versions of the hands-on experiments I did with my students in the classroom. The first task at the science center was to set up our own workshop to fabricate exhibits. To fill the hall until we could make our own, we bought some exhibits from the Exploratorium. I believe those were the first exhibits the Exploratorium replicated for sale. Nowadays this has become an important branch of their enterprise.

Making interactive exhibits. The task of thinking up exhibits, designing, developing, and testing them was both expensive and time-consuming. So, early on, a group of museums formed a collaborative in which each member-museum developed an exhibition and then sent it traveling to the other members. This way we could take a couple of years to produce our own exhibition and in the meantime would be hosting several different exhibitions for our public. This was a wonderful arrangement. For our first exhibition, 'About Faces,' we worked with Paul Ekman, from San Francisco, who has done fascinating work on the universality of certain facial expressions. We also worked with Ed Tannenbaum, who had developed a mirror/TV monitor/computer arrangement that allowed visitors to manipulate their own faces in a variety of ways. There were, of course, several other craftspeople involved, including Paul Avery, designer and fabricator superstar, who worked with me throughout the science center days. Our first exhibition covered 1500 square feet. Our second, Symmetry, was 3,000 square feet. Our third, Signals, developed with my own NSF grant, was 4.500 square feet. As we grew in expertise, the size of the exhibition we could invent and produce became larger.

Why was this work so satisfying? Mostly because it entailed a great deal of creativity: dreaming up the topic, deciding what phenomena and concepts to use in presenting it, choosing the relevant activities. In addition, the creativity needed to be paired with knowledge of the subject matter and enough expertise to make the whole hang together (rather than exhibiting a set of isolated, disconnected instances). Furthermore, the fabrication of the exhibits required hands-on experience to be able to discuss implementation with the builders. Aesthetic considerations also played a role in the looks of the stations. Finally, leadership was needed to make the group function harmoniously and to keep budget and timeline constraints. I felt particularly competent in these areas and enjoyed the whole process. What's more, the exhibitions were very successful: they traveled, not only to the museums in the collaborative, but also to Canada, Europe, and Israel; some were duplicated for sale in response to museum requests.

GF had all these maxims that his students collected. One of them was: "wood is not a laboratory material." Glass, metal, and plastic are suitable: they don't change size with the weather. The manipulative part of the exhibits, then, was made of glass, metal, and plastic. But the furniture that encased them was usually wood. Paul Avery would talk to me of white wood (birch) and dark wood (walnut), of soft wood (pine) and hard wood (oak), of routing to give shape, and finishing to seal. Wood was a whole world. When I left the museum I enrolled in a woodworking program. I became a freshman with a PhD. I loved working wood with the electric saws, the chisels, the plane. I made an arts-and-crafts style night table for Shoshanah's house; a mailbox; some artsy boxes. It lasted three years: I was a good student but did not graduate.

Using exhibits for research on learning. The science center proved to be a good laboratory for continuing the research agenda I had started at the university. Instead of using the college students as subjects, we used the museum visitors. The interactive exhibits encourage visitors to experiment freely with natural phenomena; this provides a unique setting for studying how people learn. The way we went about it was to establish protocols for eliciting the ideas that visitors brought with them; this was mostly accomplished by asking for predictions about what would happen if they did this or that at the exhibit. Then they got to try it out, in order to test their prediction. The next step was a conversation about what had actually happened and how it could be explained. With this methodology, using a variety of exhibits, we studied children's conceptions of light and vision — formation of images, shadows, colors — and showed how the children use these notions in a consistent manner to interpret the phenomena they manipulate and observe. At the time, this was a field in its infancy. By now it has blossomed.

The Argentina connection

The darwinios. In 1998, through a very good friend in Argentina, Clara Mallar, I met a group of young biologists who had wanted to set up an interactive museum on human evolution; they had received a grant from the Fundación Antorchas to develop prototypes of exhibits. No one in the group had any experience with interactive museums, and I was delighted to serve as mentor for the project. They constituted themselves into a formal association called Darwinia, so I refer to each member of the group as a 'darwinio'; this is useful when talking to other friends of mine who do not know them individually. Over the course of the past twenty years they have gone their separate ways, but I have remained in close touch with Federico Geller, Sebastian Preliasco, Leandro Panetta, Melina Furman, Gabriel Gellon, and Diego Golombek.

The project on human evolution was long and laborious. The darwinios had a lot to learn about exhibit development, and learn they did. In the end, the project was reduced to one hall in the existing museum of natural history in Buenos Aires, the Bernardino Rivadavia. It was an excellent exhibition; unfortunately, it has deteriorated because upkeep is difficult and minimal in a funds-strapped country.

Expedición Ciencia. While the darwinios were still working on the human evolution exhibition — and after I returned to the USA — I learned that one of their group was in San Diego: Gabriel. I'd not met him before and now, as chance would have it, we were in the same city. We started meeting once a week in a coffee house — argentinian style. Gabriel had just graduated from UCSD and had begun teaching high-school-level science. I shared with him my science teaching philosophy, and class notes and materials that he could use in his classes. We also discussed the human evolution exhibition in Buenos Aires, receiving updates from the darwinios and sharing ideas with them.

I am proud that Gabriel says he was my graduate student and got an informal degree in science education working with me. He was planning to return to Argentina and dreamed of setting up a camp for hands-on science learning. Much of the material we were discussing was suitable for use in an informal environment such as an outdoor camp.

Upon his return to Argentina, Gabriel started Expedición Ciencia, a summer camp in beautiful Bariloche, for adolescent students recruited from the whole country. Expedición Ciencia has done extremely well; it has expanded its offerings and is now taught and partially run by its own graduates of prior years. A true success story.

The Egyptian Hall in La Plata. Sometime in the early 2000s I went with some friends to visit the Museum of Natural History in La Plata. About one hour by bus or car from Buenos Aires, La Plata is the capital city of the Province of Buenos Aires. Its natural history museum is a magnificent edifice from the late 1800s, built to house the paleontological specimens that were being unearthed at the time; these included mastodons and glyptodonts, discovered by the Ameghino brothers and by Darwin himself in his voyage on the Beagle.

My friends and I had gone to see the Aksha Hall where the objects that had been brought back by my father from his archeological digs in Sudan were displayed. To our dismay the Hall was closed. The head of the archeology section opened it for us, and explained that it had been closed to visitors because the stones were deteriorating. He thought it was due to lack of climate control. I asked if I could look into obtaining a grant to install climate control. He agreed. So when I got back to the USA I applied to the Getty Foundation, which, I knew, helped countries preserve their antiquities. In fact we did get a grant from the Getty, but they said it would be to pay for the services of an expert to evaluate the reason for the deterioration of the stones, determine how it could be stopped and remedied, and train the local staff in future preservation. It seemed a wonderful plan. My father's student, Perla Fuscaldo, made contact with egyptologists in the USA and was given the name of a free-lance conservator from Boston, Kent Severson.

Kent proved to be a real find. He was extremely competent, intelligent, got along well with everybody. He determined that the problem was that the sandstone had been painted over with an epoxy to protect it; but over time the epoxy flaked and carried the sand particles with it. The thing to do was to get rid of the epoxy — laboriously, with q-tips and acetone — and leave the stone bare as it had been in the desert for thousands of years. The epoxy treatment was usual in the 1960s; it had been done after consultation with the egyptology museum in Leiden. Luckily the remedy was simple.

Aksha Hall was on the ground floor of the museum, in the midst of the paleontology section. It should have gone to the floor above, where the anthropological exhibits were housed, but there had been doubts as to whether the floor could carry the load since many of the pieces were huge and heavy. Thirty years later, when we started the work with the Getty grant, engineers were brought in to determine the strength of the floor and it was declared sufficiently strong. So it was resolved to move the exhibition. Dismounting the pieces from where they were was quite a job: they had been cemented to the wall and to the floor. Special equipment was brought in, cranes from the nearby port of Quilmes, to deal with the 1.5-ton column from the governor's palace. The move was quite a spectacle: the pieces were lovingly wrapped and laid on cradles specially assembled; they exited the hall through a window, traveled around the building, and were hoisted 50 feet with a crane to enter the new hall through a window. The pieces were then mounted using modern reversible techniques.

There exists documentation of much of the project: a movie of the dismantling of the old exhibition on the ground floor and the process of packaging and transporting and hoisting — in particular the column of the palace of the governor — to the upper floor. And there are the final reports by Kent Severson to the Getty Foundation on the conservation work done. In addition, there is a story-line book with drawings, photos, and captions of the new script for the exhibition and its new floor plan that we developed with darwinios Sebastian and Federico. (The old exhibition captions had been fairly academic, as was usual in the 1970s. The new captions and organization followed modern pedagogical principles and rules, and were designed to be visitor friendly.)

Some other egyptian pieces already owned by the museum were added to the hall, and it was renamed the Egyptian Hall with the byline: 'Fragments of history on the shores of the Nile.' For the duration of the project, when I was not in Argentina the museum curator and I had long weekly conversations via Skype. It took six years of effort until the Egyptian Hall was inaugurated in 2013. It is beautiful and popular, a tribute to, and legacy from, my father, who initiated egyptological studies in Argentina. But what remains beyond this accomplishment are the personal relationships developed and the deep sense of excitement and fulfillment derived from a complex project carried to fruition.

As an addendum to the large exhibition project, one of the team members, Sebastian, is now working with me on a book: an illustrated story of the argentinian archeological expedition led by my father. As is always the case when one finishes a large undertaking, and I'm referring here to the development of the Egyptian Hall, there is much material that has not made its way into the final version. We have visuals — slides and photos — of the campaigns and stories shared in letters written by my parents from the field; we are digitizing these materials and hope to use them to tell stories as yet untold.

A science museum in Buenos Aires. Yet another museum project I worked on is the National Science Museum inaugurated in 2016. This museum is housed in a modern, elegant new building that also hosts the recently founded Ministerio de Ciencia y Tecnología (a Ministerio is equivalent to a Department of the executive branch of the federal government). The idea of building a modern museum of science was long-standing. The first attempt took place in the 1980s and got as far as producing a complete set of architectural plans for a lovely site next to the river (Rio de la Plata) and scheduling traveling exhibitions from the USA. This effort was spearheaded by my math professor, Manuel Sadosky, who held the position of head of Science and Technology — at the time, a section of the Department of Education. I was involved in this project, which ended when then-president Alfonsin was forced to resign. Years later I participated in another attempt to develop a museum of science, starting from scratch. In 2012, darwinio Diego was put in charge of developing the now-existing new museum. I consulted heavily during its development, mostly via Skype. I'm afraid I don't think the result of this effort is particularly successful.

Books. Together with darwinios Gabriel, Melina, and Diego we have written a book for docents about teaching as we do, with a hands-on, process-based approach. This book, 'La ciencia en el aula,' is widely used by secondary school teachers in all of Latin America. I also contributed two books to a collection directed by Diego, made up of books for the lay person, written by scientists. My first book, 'Cielito Lindo,' is based on a unit I used to teach at SDSU: naked-eye astronomy. The second book is 'Simetría,' based on the exhibition we developed at the Reuben Fleet Science Center, capitalizing on the years of research and materials accumulated on the topic.

Closing a life that makes sense

Six months after GF's death I went to Buenos Aires, my usual bi-annual spring-here-autumn-there trip. One item on the agenda was settling the upkeep of my affairs since it was clear my brother, because of his deteriorating health, couldn't be in charge any longer. The other item was the presentation of the new edition of 'La ciencia en el aula'; Melina, always active, had arranged for this presentation to happen during my trip. At that time she introduced me to Gerry Garbulsky, who runs TEDX Rio de la Plata, and asked me to give a TED talk. We met at the Zurich, the corner café that is my ersatz dining-conference room. I told Gerry I don't give talks anymore — I'm not interested in talking about education, or symmetry, or museums. But he is sharp, convincing, and a fellow physicist. So when he asked what I am thinking about these days, and I said "closing off projects" and mentioned the metaphor of life as a project of projects, he said "ah, a fractal view of life." And that did it: he understood, he focused on a topic that was timely for me, and I accepted the challenge. The fractals eventually dropped out of the talk — too technical a concept — but not from the way I think.

The TED event was to take place six months after this initial meeting. In the protocol for these talks the speaker is assigned a mentor whose job it is to help out and monitor the end result. There are also a couple of rehearsals where the other speakers and mentors give feedback. This is not too different from the way we used to prepare for the ten-minute talks that are standard at physics conferences. I was assigned two mentors: darwinios Melina and Leandro. Twenty years earlier I had been <u>their</u> mentor on a science exhibition project in Buenos Aires. It felt like I was being tossed a lifesaver in my time of need: a project with collaborators dear to my heart, as well as a chance to review my life at a critical moment.

It was a healing experience. My two mentors offered me mirrors, angled to reflect my professional life as it impacted them. Melina, who has forged for herself a distinguished career in science education, reflected for me the Sputnik experience. Leandro is a designer of large-scale interpretations of nature and history, in the form of creative plays, and happenings at the site of monuments; he reflected for me the interactive science museum experience.

Sputnik, as I say in the talk, was the first artificial satellite. Melina reminds me that seeing it in 1957 meant witnessing a historic moment. The launch of a new world, no less. Before satellites there could be no cell phones, those devices that seem to be life itself to most people nowadays. Without satellites there would be no GPS that allows you to determine and communicate your location and move about with ease. Also, because Sputnik was russian and the USA competed with Russia in the race for space, the launch of Sputnik engendered an educational reform in the USA. Without the cold war the educational reform might not have happened the way it did, with so much federal funding. And my engagement in new ways of teaching science might never have taken place.

The interactive science centers were being invented in the 1980s. Leandro says: "When I mention you I say you were one of the founders of the interactive museum movement." Leandro remembers my maxims: "One exhibit, one message," "time and budget: multiply your estimate by pi (3.1416)." And yes, it's true. I just hadn't thought of myself that way. Pioneering.

This is the TED talk I gave in the Teatro Colón in Buenos Aires on November 5, 2018[2]:

Closing a life that makes sense

When there is a critical moment in our lives, we look ahead and we look back. We look ahead to gauge what we are up against: How are we going to face it? We look backwards to assess how we have lived until now and how this past helps us live our future.

My critical moment is now. A few months ago my husband died, my partner for 60 years. I did not think I would find widowhood so difficult. True, the roots of two trees intertwine when they have grown together for so many years. But that was not the problem. I think what happened has another, different metaphor: We were side by side on a diving board, and when I found myself alone, without him, I was left without the impulse, the synchronous vibration that helped launch us into the world of projects and adventure.

I look backwards and I see my whole life, very long and complete. I look forwards and see the need to button up, close off, finish. This is what I want to talk to you about: the meaning and importance of closing. I will do so using as examples some projects from my life.

In October 1957, from the rooftop of my apartment house in New York, I watched Sputnik — the first artificial satellite, which had just been put in space by the Russians. It passed overhead every 90 minutes. I had just arrived in the States from Argentina, newly graduated from the University of Buenos Aires, to study at Columbia University.

My husband-to-be — whom I did not yet know — was working against the clock in the development of a maser (a quantum amplifier) that would go in the first USA artificial satellite. This satellite was launched in January, too late to win the race for space: The Soviet Union had successfully put Sputnik in orbit three months earlier.

---

[2] It is online at http://amara.org/et/videos/9Co9kguzG7o5/en/2350637

Sputnik unleashed a whirlwind in the USA: what was wrong with science in the US if the Soviets had won the race to space? With great speed funds were approved by Congress for the best minds in the country to undertake a radical reform of science education: Young people should receive better training so the US could beat Russia. The educational reform became a huge project of the entire country and it marked my professional career.

Traditional science education — this is how I was taught — presented science as a set of laws — the laws of Newton, for example — that had been handed down to us much the way God handed the tablets of the law to Moses. By contrast, the multitude of post-Sputnik projects sought to present science as a process, similar to the one that scientists engage in when they work. The idea was that students should carry out small scientific projects: observing phenomena and asking themselves how they can be explained; formulating hypotheses and seeing how they can be confirmed — or not. You have a fistful of sodium bicarbonate; you pour some vinegar on it; bubbles are produced; what are those bubbles? can I trap them in a container? And if I do, what happens if I light a match? Does the flame grow bigger, go out, stay the same? Can I give a name to this gas?

My role in this post-Sputnik effort was to develop courses for prospective teachers in which science was taught through activities such as the one I just described. This went hand-in-hand with research on students' ideas and how to help them evolve and learn.

This portion of my life is way behind me. If I think about how these projects were closed, I see it was a matter of having trained people, built a following and passed on the torch. Because the basic philosophy, the activities, the results of the research, all of it continues alive in the professional tasks of young colleagues.

Some time later it became clear that this wave of reform in science education was gathering momentum and propagating out of the classrooms on to zoos, summer camps, museums. I surfed the wave into an interactive museum that we founded in the 1980s in California. An interactive museum is a place where the exhibits are <u>not</u> valuable objects but, rather, interesting phenomena, presented as activities for the visitor to explore. What is valuable is the phenomenon. Interactive museums exist now all over. At the time we were inventing them from scratch.

In the museum we developed several exhibitions that ended up traveling throughout North America, Europe and beyond. Each exhibition was a completed project with the specific characteristics of a project. Namely: You begin with an idea followed by an overflow of ideas. Some of them blossom, others lead nowhere, some follow unexpected paths, others appear by chance. But at a certain moment the money runs out; or the time. So you start trimming: This costs too much, we don't have the funds; this takes too long, we won't be able to finish it. And so you let go, button up, close off until the show finally opens.

Closing this kind of project means achieving a final product that is launched into the world: a show that opens, a book that is published, a child that is born. A TED talk that is given. (And believe me, a TED talk is no mean endeavor.)

Looking at my life, I realized that if I scratch a little here I discover a project. And if I scratch there I discover another project — maybe big, maybe small, but something that opened up, blossomed, and, with luck, closed up. I have this vision of my life as a large tree, a pine perhaps, that gives off branches and the branches give off needles and the whole thing grows and opens up and tops off at the crown. And there is the structure, the whole tree, made up of branches and needles. But if you look at the detail, you see that each branch is also made up of branches and needles. Everything in the tree is similar, the detail and the tree itself: a large project that opens up and closes off, made up of an infinity of projects each of which opens up and closes off.

So then: If my life is a large project of projects, as it opened up so also must it close off. Which means that in my octogenarian life it is no longer the time to open up new projects but to close off those that are still open.

I'm in the midst of projects that round off lives that are dear to me. For example, we are preparing a book on the archeological mission that my father led in the 1960s to the area of the world that was Ancient Egypt. From those excavations he brought to Argentina pieces that are on display in the Egyptian wing of the Natural History Museum of La Plata. That exhibition hall is now open to the public. But, to close off my part in this project, I need to do the book.

Why is it so important to close off? If we do not bring projects to a close, the ideas get lost. We bring to a close in order to give ideas the necessary form that enables them to survive. Not to bury and forget. The Egyptians themselves, when they mummified and buried, it was, precisely, to enable the dead to survive in the world beyond. Seen in this light, closing off is an act of liberation.

Returning to the image of the pine tree, the large project made up of projects: With a bit of luck it sends off seeds that fall on fertile ground and breed a forest of pines. That would be immortality. But for me, what is truly important is my pine, my life. To be able to look at a structure that is harmonious and coherent; to be able to say: "I close my life and my life makes sense."

To close a life and end up with a life that makes sense is a lot of work! But it is work that is worthwhile because it gives meaning to living day by day.

The infinite project?

The beauty of this project, writing the weave of my life, is that it doesn't really have an end. So long as I find stories to tell I can keep on adding strands to the weft, making the weave tighter. This lets me dream as if I were to live forever, and live as if I were to die tomorrow… until I do.